More Family Storytimes

Twenty-four Creative Programs for All Ages

Rob Reid

American Library Association
Chicago   2009

Rob Reid is a full-time instructor at the University of Wisconsin–Eau Claire specializing in children's literature and literature for adolescents. He is the author of several ALA Editions books, including *Family Storytime, Something Funny Happened at the Library, Cool Story Programs for the School-Age Crowd, Children's Jukebox,* and *Something Musical Happened at the Library.* He has a regular column in *Book Links* magazine titled "The Reid-Aloud Alert" and is a regular contributor to *LibrarySparks* magazine. He is a recent recipient of the Wisconsin Librarian of the Year. In addition to teaching and writing, Reid visits schools and libraries as a children's humorist, using storytelling, musical activities, and wordplay to make reading come alive for children.

The paper used in this publication meets the minimum requirements of American National Standard for Information Sciences—Permanence of Paper for Printed Library Materials, ANSI Z39.48-1992. ∞

Library of Congress Cataloging-in-Publication Data
Reid, Rob.
  More family storytimes : twenty-four creative programs for all ages / Rob Reid.
    p. cm.
  Includes bibliographical references and index.
    ISBN 978-0-8389-0973-7 (alk. paper)
    1. Storytelling—United States. 2. Children's libraries—Activity programs—United States. 3. Libraries and families—United States. I. Title.
Z718.3.R46 2009
027.62'51—dc22   2008015377

ISBN-13: 978-0-8389-0973-7

Printed in the United States of America
13   12   11   10   09   5   4   3   2   1

To my brother, David, my sister, Susan,
and the memory of our parents,
Eldo Fountain Reid and Helen Mary Goff Reid

Contents

Acknowledgments

Family is very important to me. I couldn't do what I do without my wife, Jayne, and our children, Laura, Julia, Alice, and Sam. I also get my battery charged from Steven, Daphne, Betty, Janine, Mark, Kevin, Steven, Jodi, Mike, Jennifer, Jim, Andy, Michael, Hannah, Julianne, Dave, Jean, Bob, Katie, Eric, Elizabeth, and Matt—as well as my brother, David, and my sister, Susan—to whom I dedicate this book.

Friends are very important to me. Thanks to Shawn and Rhonda for keeping me connected. Thanks to Barbara, Carol, Dwight, Gail, Jane, the Jills, Katherine, Mark, Roger, and Tamara for the daily support and excitement. Thanks to Claudia, Colleen, David, Georgia, Kate, Kati, Marge, Milton, Shu, and Sonia for being part of my music and library family.

I thank the following for permission to use their published material:

Jayne Freij for permission to reprint the lyrics of "R-I-N-G-O."

Monty Harper for permission to reprint part of the lyrics to "Lisa Lee Elizabeth." Monty Harper Productions, 1996.

Upstart Books for "I'm Not Sleepy," movement activity by Rob Reid originally published in "I Don't Want to Go to Sleep," on pages 45–48 of *LibrarySparks* magazine, vol. 5, no. 4. Reprinted with permission of Upstart, a division of Highsmith Inc. All rights reserved.

Introduction

It's been a decade since I wrote *Family Storytime* (ALA Editions, 1999). The response from the youth services library profession was extremely supportive, so much so that ALA Editions asked me to write this book. Although I am no longer a practicing librarian, I find myself in front of dozens of family groups each year, entertaining them with stories and songs at libraries, schools, festivals, and literacy programs.

I thoroughly enjoy audiences where young children are joined by older siblings, parents, grandparents, cousins, and friends. This is in sharp contrast to my first introduction to public library story programs, in the early 1980s. I volunteered at my local library and was told, "Whatever you do, don't let the parents in!" The mind-set was that the parents were disruptive and the children needed to learn independence. I followed orders—for a while. Then I let one parent sneak in. I enjoyed her presence. She got into the stories and was able to interact in a positive literary manner with her child. I let another parent in . . . and another. It was about this time that I got my first job as a youth services librarian, at the Pueblo (CO) Library District. I created the library's first family story program. We had two families attend. By the time I left Pueblo, two years later, we had crowds of eighty in attendance on a regular basis. I moved to Eau Claire, Wisconsin, and began a new series of family story programs there as well. Today, I can't imagine conducting a story program without adult family members in the audience.

As I mentioned in the introduction to *Family Storytime,* "When parents and caregivers are present, the enjoyment and educational aspects of the story program are heightened. The adults become positive role models for the children for reading, reading-readiness activities, and becoming lifelong library users. Adults learn proper techniques for reading aloud. They learn stories, fingerplays, songs, and activities. They remember stories, songs, and fingerplays from their own childhood and are thrilled to learn new ones."

There is a greater pool of resources available for an intergenerational story program—from picture books to movement activities, from songs to crafts—than what is available for a traditional preschool storytime. Authors such as Doreen Cronin, Margie Palatini, Adam Rex, Jon Scieszka, and Mo Willems consciously speak to the adults in their picture books. The child will enjoy the story at one level, older children will pick up some aspects the younger children will miss, and the adults will catch all types of humor and sophistication not normally associated with children's ware.

My approach to this book was to revisit the first *Family Storytime* book and update the same twenty-four themes, featuring, with only a few exceptions, books and recordings published between 1998 and 2008. The last decade has been a rich period for both children's books and children's music. To supplement these print and audio resources, I sampled liberally from older traditional camp songs and activities. I learned many from my Children's Literature students at the University of Wisconsin–Eau Claire. Camp counselors have a wealth of musical and movement activities. I altered some to fit the different program themes. I also wrote a lot of original material to fit a particular gap between two picture books in a program. I encourage everyone to create their own original material or set new words to traditional songs. All of the material in this book has been kid-tested, mom-tested, and dad-tested with various groups around the country.

I open each chapter with a "Program at a Glance." I like having these lists on hand when I give a presentation to keep the overall program in mind. The program itself is detailed in "Preparation and Presentation." I chose an opening song for each theme. I like to play music as families enter the story program area. I often find that an adult will walk up to learn the name of the artist. Once the program begins, I like to have a lively mix of picture books and supplemental activities, such as fingerplays, music, movement activities, and poetry. I also like to choose picture books that lend themselves to audience participation, usually with the audience members providing sound effects. I typically construct the program so that the more active stories and songs occur near the end of the program and the quieter, longer pieces are shared near the beginning. The "Mix and Match" section features additional picture books and recorded songs that fit each theme. I encourage you to alter these programs to play to your strengths. Many of the children's books in this book fit more than one theme. For example, David Shannon's *No, David!* is found in "The Name Game" chapter. It also fits well in "Super Moms, Super Grandmas, and Super Aunts" and "Uh-Oh! Accidents!" Consider taking some of the older material from *Family Storytime* and blending it with the programs found in this book.

The themes themselves are timeless. The first theme is titled "Second-Generation Favorites." I chose to stick with traditional folk stories and folk songs this time around with this particular theme. The second theme, "Altered Endings and Twisted Tales," complements the first chapter. These are parodies of long-standing stories. One of my favorite themes is titled "Mouthsounds." It's all about making sound effects. I like my programs to be noisy and active. The remaining chapters cover topics and concepts that are very popular in children's literature.

I'd like to end this introduction with another quote from *Family Storytime:* "I liken family storytimes to family reunions. Many families have busy schedules and are hard-pressed to have time together." By offering a family story program series, you will be a valuable partner creating many memories for many families.

A New Hello

In *Family Storytime,* I shared an opening ditty, "Some of These Stories," that can be used with any story program theme. I have a new utility opening for this book. It can be sung to any melody that pops into your head. Have the audience repeat each line after you.

"Hello, Kids!" by Rob Reid

> Hello, kids!   (Hello, kids!)
> Moms and Dads!   (Moms and Dads!)
> And everyone else!   (And everyone else!)
> And everyone else!   (And everyone else!)

Repeat it a few more times: high-pitched, low voice, "doggy" voice ("woof-woof-woof"), "under water" voice (sing while running fingers over lips), loud voice, whisper, and finally silently mouth the words.

THE PROGRAMS

Second-Generation Favorites

PROGRAM AT A GLANCE

Opening Song: "Polly Wolly Doodle" from *Rocket Ship Beach* by Dan Zanes
Picture Book: *Goldilocks and the Three Bears* by Carolyn Buehner
Song: "The ABC Song/Baa, Baa, Black Sheep/Twinkle, Twinkle, Little Star,"
    traditional
Picture Book: *Glass Slipper, Gold Sandal: A Worldwide Cinderella* by Paul Fleischman
Musical Activity: "I'm a Little Teapot," traditional
Picture Book: *This Is the House That Jack Built* by Simms Taback
Movement Activity: "Brow Bender," traditional
Picture Book: *The Boy Who Cried Wolf* by B. G. Hennessy
Clapping Activity: "Miss Mary Mack," traditional
Readers' Theater: "The Little Red Hen and the Grain of Wheat" from *You Read
    to Me, I'll Read to You: Very Short Fairy Tales to Read Together* by Mary Ann
    Hoberman
Musical Activity: "This Old Man," traditional

PREPARATION AND PRESENTATION

Opening Song

**"Polly Wolly Doodle." From *Rocket Ship Beach*, by Dan Zanes. Festival Five
Records, 2000.**

Dan Zanes, former member of the rock group Del Fuegos, is one of the
brightest stars on the children's music scene. In addition to a few original songs,
Zanes brings life to old, traditional music, such as this popular song here.

Picture Book

Goldilocks and the Three Bears, by Carolyn Buehner. Illustrated by Mark Buehner. Dial, 2007.

This traditional folktale has nice little touches by author Buehner. For example, when Little Wee Bear tastes his breakfast, he tries to say that his porridge is too hot. But, "because his mouth was so full it sounded like: 'My porch has a bus light.'" Mark Buehner also adds nice artistic touches, such as having a poster of Smokey the Bear on the bears' bedroom wall and depicting Goldilocks as barely visible in the chair that's too soft. Goldilocks herself is very personable and energetic with her jump rope.

Song

"The ABC Song/Baa, Baa, Black Sheep/Twinkle, Twinkle, Little Star," traditional.

Point out that all three of these popular children's songs have the same melody. Sing one after the other.

ABCDEFG, HIJKLMNOP, QRS, TUV, WX, Y and Z,
Now I know my ABCs.
Next time won't you sing with me?
Baa, baa, black sheep,
Have you any wool?
Yes sir, yes sir, three bags full.
One for my master, one for my dame,
And one for the little boy who lives down the lane.
Baa, baa, black sheep,
Have you any wool,
Yes sir, yes sir, three bags full.
Twinkle, twinkle, little star,
How I wonder what you are,
Up above the world so high,
Like a diamond in the sky.
Twinkle, twinkle, little star,
How I wonder what you are.

Picture Book

Glass Slipper, Gold Sandal: A Worldwide Cinderella, by Paul Fleischman. Illustrated by Julie Paschkis. Holt, 2007.

Fleischman wove together many segments of Cinderella variants found around the world. The country of origin for each segment or phrase is identified in the illustrations. Ask a volunteer to stand or sit near you and state each country before you read that particular phrase. The story flows beautifully while the audience hears the similarities and differences of the many versions. Here's an example: Russia: "Then she reached into the hole in the birch tree"; Indonesia: "Then a crocodile swam up to the surface, and in its mouth was a sarong made of gold"; China: "a cloak sewn of kingfisher feathers"; Japan: "a kimono red as sunset"; France: "And on the girl's feet appeared a pair of glass slippers."

Musical Activity

"I'm a Little Teapot," traditional.
 Ask everyone to stand and act out the motions.

> I'm a little teapot, short and stout,
> Here is my handle, here is my spout,   *(one hand on hip, other arm point out)*
> When I get all steamed up, then I shout
> Tip me over and pour me out.   *(lean over)*

Picture Book

***This Is the House That Jack Built,* by Simms Taback. Putnam, 2002.**
 Jack builds a multilevel, oddly structured house and fills it with cheese. We encounter a rat, a cat, a dog, a cow, a maiden, a man, a judge, a rooster, a farmer, and, finally, an artist who resembles Taback. The last picture shows someone tossing the cheese out a window. Let the audience pore over the many details found throughout the book (and back cover) at the end of the program.

Movement Activity

"Brow Bender," traditional.
 Here is an old variation of a popular nursery rhyme. Everyone can do this while sitting.

> Brow bender,   *(point to forehead)*
> Eye peeper,   *(point to eyes)*
> Nose dropper,   *(point to nose)*
> Mouth eater,   *(point to mouth)*
> Chin chopper,   *(point to chin)*
> Knock at the door,   *(tickle under chin)*
> Ring the bell,   *(tug at ear)*

Lift up the latch,   *(slightly raise nose)*

Walk in,   *(suck thumb)*

Take a chair,

Sit there,   *(fold hands in lap)*

And how do you do this morning?   *(raise hand as if to shake someone else's hand)*

Picture Book

The Boy Who Cried Wolf, **by B. G. Hennessy. Illustrated by Boris Kulikov. Simon & Schuster, 2006.**

A shepherd boy becomes extremely bored while watching his sheep. The audience can chime in on the sheep's repetitive phrase, "'Munch, munch, munch. Baaaaaaaaaaaaaa,' answered the sheep." The boy yells that a wolf is after the sheep to add a little excitement to his day. The townsfolk fall for it. The boy next cries that two wolves are after his sheep. Same results. The next day, the boy hears a different sound. "Lunch, lunch, lunch! Grrrrrrrrrrrrrrrrrrrrrr." (The audience can make this sound, too.) The sheep scatter, and the shepherd has no clue where they went. The audience will enjoy spotting the sheep high overhead in a tree.

Clapping Activity

"Miss Mary Mack," traditional.

Have everyone stand and face a partner. Many of the mothers in the room may be familiar with this classic jump-rope and clapping chant. There are many clapping patterns. Here's one:

1. Cross hands across chest on "Miss."
2. Place hands on legs on "Mar-"
3. Clap your own hands on "-y."
4. Clap your hand with your partner's opposite hand, clap your hands, and repeat two more times.
5. Start over.

Miss Mary Mack, Mack, Mack,

All dressed in black, black, black,

With silver buttons, buttons, buttons,

All down her back, back, back.

She asked her mother, mother, mother,

For fifty cents, cents, cents,

To watch an elephant, elephant, elephant,

Jump over the fence, fence, fence.

He jumped so high, high, high,

He reached the sky, sky, sky,

And he never came back, back, back,

Till the fourth of July, July, July.

Readers' Theater

"The Little Red Hen and the Grain of Wheat." From *You Read to Me, I'll Read to You: Very Short Fairy Tales to Read Together,* by Mary Ann Hoberman. Little, Brown, 2004.

Ask for four volunteers from the audience to read this traditional story retold in verse. Hoberman has already laid out the parts of the Little Red Hen, the Duck, the Cat, and the Dog in the text. The Duck, the Cat, and the Dog can read their lines together for most of the second half of the script. Divide their lines for the following sequence: "What story is that, Hen?" "And what is it called, Hen?" and "Why, that sounds like you, Hen."

Musical Activity

"This Old Man," traditional.

Teach the audience the following hand movements and then ask them to sing along. On "knick-knack," clap legs twice; on "paddy whack," clap hands twice; and on "this old man came rolling home," have everyone twirl their hands around each other.

This old man, he played one, 　 *(hold up thumb)*

He played knick-knack on my thumb, 　 *(tap thumb with other hand)*

With a knick-knack, paddy whack,

Give a dog a bone,

This old man came rolling home.

This old man, he played two, 　 *(hold up two fingers)*

He played knick-knack on my shoe, 　 *(tap shoe)*

With a knick-knack, paddy whack,

Give a dog a bone,

This old man came rolling home.

This old man, he played three,   *(hold up three fingers)*
He played knick-knack on my knee,   *(tap knee)*
With a knick-knack, paddy whack,
Give a dog a bone,
This old man came rolling home.

This old man, he played four,   *(hold up four fingers)*
He played knick-knack on my door,   *(imitate knocking)*
With a knick-knack, paddy whack,
Give a dog a bone,
This old man came rolling home.

This old man, he played five,   *(hold up five fingers)*
He played knick-knack on my hive,   *(flutter hands about head to
    simulate a swarm of bees)*
With a knick-knack, paddy whack,
Give a dog a bone,
This old man came rolling home.

This old man, he played six,   *(hold up six fingers)*
He played knick-knack on my sticks,   *(mime picking up sticks)*
With a knick-knack, paddy whack,
Give a dog a bone,
This old man came rolling home.

This old man, he played seven,   *(hold up seven fingers)*
He played knick-knack up in heaven,   *(point upward)*
With a knick-knack, paddy whack,
Give a dog a bone,
This old man came rolling home.

This old man, he played eight,   *(hold up eight fingers)*
He played knick-knack on my gate,   *(mime swinging a gate open and shut)*
With a knick-knack, paddy whack,
Give a dog a bone,
This old man came rolling home.

This old man, he played nine,   *(hold up nine fingers)*
He played knick-knack on my spine,   *(reach around and tap back)*
With a knick-knack, paddy whack,
Give a dog a bone,
This old man came rolling home.

This old man, he played ten,   *(hold up all ten fingers)*
He played knick-knack once again,   *(twirl one finger in the air)*
With a knick-knack, paddy whack,
Give a dog a bone,
This old man came rolling home.

MIX AND MATCH

Additional Picture Books

Andersen, Hans Christian. *The Ugly Ducking*. Illustrated by Jerry Pinkney. Morrow, 1999.
   A duck notices that one of her eggs is larger than the others. She is surprised by the size of the chick that hatches from the egg. She tries to protect it from taunting ducks, but they drive the young bird away. The duckling spends the winter alone. In the spring, the duckling sees a flock of beautiful swans and realizes he is one of them.

Aylesworth, Jim. *Aunt Pitty Patty's Piggy*. Illustrated by Barbara McClintock. Scholastic, 1999.
   Aunt Pitty Patty and her niece Nelly buy a piggy and take it home. The piggy refuses to go through the gate, so Nelly runs for help. She asks a dog to bite piggy, but the dog refuses. She asks a stick to hit dog, a fire to burn stick, water to douse fire, an ox to drink water, a butcher to scare ox, a rope to tie butcher, a mouse to gnaw rope, and a cat to chase rat. The cat agrees only if Nellie brings milk. A cow exchanges the milk for hay, which a farmer gives Nellie in exchange for supper with Aunt Pitty Patty. This sets off a chain reaction that eventually makes piggy go through the gate.

Demi. *The Emperor's New Clothes*. McElderry, 2000.
   Demi set this traditional tale in China and stayed true to the story line. Two travelers convince the Imperial Emperor that they can make magical clothes: clothing so magical that "only clever people can see them. Fools cannot." The emperor walks among his people in his undergarments. No one can see the

magical clothes, but they are afraid to say anything and reveal they are fools. It takes a young child to point out the real fools. Ask your audience to join the refrain, "No, no, no, I will not go!"

Pinkney, Jerry. *The Little Red Hen*. Dial, 2006.

The little red hen finds some strange seeds and plants them. She asks the short brown dog, thin gray rat, tall black goat, and round pink pig for help. They refuse to help plant the seeds, harvest the wheat, take the grain to the mill, and bake the bread. When the bread is done, the lazy animals reply that they will help eat the bread. The hen chases them away and sets up a nice meal for her own chicks. The audience can say the animals' lines: "Not I . . ." For extra fun, find a photo of adapter-illustrator Jerry Pinkney and then show them the illustration of Mr. Miller and his drawing supplies in the mill.

Shepard, Aaron. *Master Man: A Tall Tale of Nigeria*. Illustrated by David Wisniewski. HarperCollins, 2001.

Shadusa boasts about his strength. His wife warns him, "No matter how strong you are, there will always be someone stronger. And watch out, or someday you may meet him." A baby capable of strong feats shows up. He is the son of Master Man. Shadusa is soon running for his life. A second Master Man shows up and battles the other Master Man. The two battle in the sky, and "some people call that noise thunder." Shepard has a readers' theater script of the story on his website, at www.aaronshep.com.

Additional Music Featuring Traditional Songs

Beall, Pamela, and Susan Nipp. *Wee Sing Animals, Animals, Animals*. Price Stern Sloan, 1999.

Hinton, Sam. *Whoever Shall Have Some Good Peanuts*. Smithsonian Folkways, 2006.

Kirk, John, and Trish Miller. *The Big Rock Candy Mountain*. A Gentle Wind, 2004.

Old Town School of Folk Music. *Wiggleworms Love You*. Old Town School, 2005.

Rosenthal, Phil. *Folksongs and Bluegrass for Children*. Rounder Records, 2000.

Various Artists. *Folk Playground*. Putumayo, 2006.

Altered Endings and Twisted Tales

PROGRAM AT A GLANCE

Opening Song: "Humpty Dumpty" from *I Sang It Just for You* by Mary Kaye

Picture Book: *The End* by David LaRochelle

Short Story: "Two Little Pigs" from *Once Upon a Time, the End: Asleep in 60 Seconds* by Geoffrey Kloske

Poem: "The Phantom of the Opera Can't Get 'It's a Small World' Out of His Head" from *Frankenstein Makes a Sandwich* by Adam Rex

Song: "The Farmer in the Dell," traditional

Picture Book: *The Cheese* by Margie Palatini

Poem: "The Phantom of the Opera Still Can't Get 'It's a Small World' Out of His Head" from *Frankenstein Makes a Sandwich* by Adam Rex

Chant: "The Humpty Dumpty Rap," traditional

Poem: "If The Phantom of the Opera Can't Get 'Pop Goes the Weasel' Out of His Head, He's Going to Freak Out" from *Frankenstein Makes a Sandwich* by Adam Rex

Short Story: "Goldilocks and the Bears" from *Once Upon a Time, the End: Asleep in 60 Seconds* by Geoffrey Kloske

Poem: "Now the Phantom of the Opera Can't Get 'The Girl from Ipanema' Out of His Head" from *Frankenstein Makes a Sandwich* by Adam Rex

Picture Book: *Ivan the Terrier* by Peter Catalanotto

Musical Activity: "Do Your Ears Hang Low?" traditional

Poem: "The Phantom of the Opera Is Considering Giving Up Music and Doing His Haunting Somewhere Else" from *Frankenstein Makes a Sandwich* by Adam Rex

Short Story: "Princess Pea" from *Once Upon a Time, the End: Asleep in 60 Seconds* by Geoffrey Kloske

PREPARATION AND PRESENTATION

Opening Song

"Humpty Dumpty." From *I Sang It Just for You,* by Mary Kaye. Mary Kaye Music, 2003.

A little girl worries about her imaginary friend. She tells him he need not climb up that wall. After the introduction, Mary Kaye delivers a catchy tune describing the fun the girl can have with Humpty Dumpty.

Picture Book

The End, by David LaRochelle. Illustrated by Richard Egielski. Scholastic, 2007.

Here's a fitting title to begin the story program. The book starts at "The End" and proceeds in a cumulative manner to the title page, located at the back of the book. LaRochelle takes many motifs and characters found in traditional folklore and puts a spin on them. The first sentence, "And they all lived happily ever after," shows the knight falling in love with the princess because of a chain of events that leads to the last line, "Once upon a time a clever princess decided to make a big bowl of lemonade."

Short Story

"Two Little Pigs." From *Once Upon a Time, the End: Asleep in 60 Seconds,* by Geoffrey Kloske. Illustrated by Barry Blitt. Atheneum, 2005.

The premise of this book is that a father is trying to get his child to fall asleep in a hurry by reading condensed versions of popular folktales. Scatter a few of these revised stories throughout the program. "Two Little Pigs" leaves out the little pig that built a house of sticks. After the wolf fails to blow down the house of stone, he simply leaves the forest. That's all!

Poem

"The Phantom of the Opera Can't Get 'It's a Small World' Out of His Head." From *Frankenstein Makes a Sandwich,* by Adam Rex. Harcourt, 2006.

The adults in the audience will appreciate the humor in this collection of movie-monster poems. Read and sing the musical sequence of poems that follows the woes of the Phantom of the Opera. The poem itself can be sung to the tune of "It's a Small World."

Song

"The Farmer in the Dell," traditional.

Ask the audience to join you in singing a straight version of the traditional nursery song "The Farmer in the Dell" as a prelude to the next picture book. A recording of "The Farmer in the Dell" can be found on *All-Time Children's Favorites,* by the Learning Station (Monopoli/Learning Station, 1993).

> The farmer in the dell, the farmer in the dell,
> Hi-ho the derry-o, the farmer in the dell.
> The farmer takes a wife, the farmer takes a wife,
> Hi-ho the derry-o, the farmer takes a wife.
> The wife takes a child, the wife takes a child,
> Hi-ho the derry-o, the wife takes a child.
> The child takes a dog, the child takes a dog,
> Hi-ho the derry-o, the child takes a dog.
> The dog takes a cat, the dog takes a cat,
> Hi-ho the derry-o, the dog takes a cat.
> The cat takes a rat, the cat takes a rat,
> Hi-ho the derry-o, the cat takes a rat.
> The rat takes the cheese, the rat takes the cheese,
> Hi-ho the derry-o, the rat takes the cheese.
> The cheese stands alone, the cheese stands alone,
> Hi-ho the derry-o, the cheese stands alone.

At the end of the song, ask "Why does the cheese stand alone?" Start reading the next picture book.

Picture Book

The Cheese, by Margie Palatini. Illustrated by Steve Johnson and Lou Fancher. HarperCollins, 2007.

A rat finds a chunk of cheddar cheese standing alone in the meadow. He runs toward the cheese but is joined by a cat, a dog, and a girl. The girl's mother tells them they can't eat the cheese, because "the cheese stands alone." The farmer joins them, and they all decide to have a party with the cheese and other snack items.

Poem

"The Phantom of the Opera Still Can't Get 'It's a Small World' Out of His Head." From *Frankenstein Makes a Sandwich,* by Adam Rex. Harcourt, 2006.

Everyone can sing "It's a Small World" over and over while you show the picture of the tormented Phantom of the Opera.

Chant

"The Humpty Dumpty Rap," traditional.

Have everyone stand and move to a beat as a stretching opportunity. I learned this from a student who was a camp counselor. Teach everyone to rap out a popular nursery rhyme and replace the fourth line with the phrase, "Ain't that funky now!" For some reason, the kids find this line a hundred times funnier than the adults.

> Yo! Humpty Dumpty sat on a wall,
>
> Humpty Dumpty had a great fall.
>
> All the king's horses and all the king's men said,
>
> "Ain't that funky now!"

> Yo! Jack and Jill went up a hill,
>
> To fetch a pail of water.
>
> Jack fell down and broke his crown and said,
>
> "Ain't that funky now!"

> Yo! Little Miss Muffet sat on a tuffet,
>
> Eating her curds and whey.
>
> Along came a spider, who sat down beside her, and said,
>
> "Ain't that funky now!"

> Yo! Hey, diddle diddle, the cat and the fiddle,
>
> The cow jumped over the moon.
>
> The little dog laughed to see such a sight and said,
>
> "Ain't that funky now!"

Let the audience try this formula with other simple nursery rhymes.

Poem

"If The Phantom of the Opera Can't Get 'Pop Goes the Weasel' Out of His Head, He's Going to Freak Out." From *Frankenstein Makes a Sandwich*, by Adam Rex. Harcourt, 2006.

Sing the short poem to the tune of "Pop Goes the Weasel." "All around the Opera House . . ."

Short Story

"Goldilocks and the Bears." From *Once Upon a Time, The End: Asleep in 60 Seconds,* by Geoffrey Kloske. Illustrated by Barry Blitt. Atheneum, 2005.

The father reads, "There were some bears; it doesn't really matter how many. There was a bunch." He ends by stating Goldilocks ran home to her own bed. And that "you" should go to bed, too.

Poem

"Now the Phantom of the Opera Can't Get 'The Girl from Ipanema' Out of His Head." From *Frankenstein Makes a Sandwich,* by Adam Rex. Harcourt, 2006.

The kids probably won't know "The Girl from Ipanema," but many adults will. Sing this poem, also.

Picture Book

Ivan the Terrier, by Peter Catalanotto. Atheneum, 2007.

A little dog named Ivan ruins a series of traditional folktales. As soon as we're introduced to the three goats named Gruff, Ivan runs into the picture barking and startling the goats. The narrator yells at Ivan and then begins to read "Goldilocks and the Three Bears." Ivan starts barking at the bears and upsetting the porridge. He also eats the gingerbread boy. "Oh, come on! Would somebody please grab that dog?" Ivan settles down once the narrator begins relating a story about a dog named Ivan.

Musical Activity

"Do Your Ears Hang Low?" traditional.

In my book *Family Storytime,* I relate how I was inspired to wear tights on my head while singing this song. There's even a picture of me with the tights at the end of the book. I shared new verses by the recording trio Sharon, Lois, and Bram. Since then, I've had several people tell me alternate verses of this song that they learned when they were kids. Here's the traditional song followed by a few of their offerings. Have the audience mime the motions in the lyrics.

> Do your ears hang low? Do they wobble to and fro?
> Can you tie them in a knot? Can you tie them in a bow?
> Can you throw them over your shoulder like a Continental soldier?
> Do your ears hang low?

Do your ears hang high? Do they reach up to the sky?
Do they droop when they get wet? Do they stiffen when they dry?
Can you wave them at your neighbor with a minimum of labor?
Do your ears hang high?

Do your ears flip-flop? Can you use them as a mop?
Are they stringy at the bottom? Are they curly at the top?
Can you put them in a shower with a giant daisy flower?
Do your ears flip-flop?

Does your tongue hang low? Does it wobble to and fro?
Can you tie it in a knot? Can you tie it in a bow?
Can you throw it over your shoulder like a Continental soldier?
Does your tongue hang low?

Poem

"The Phantom of the Opera Is Considering Giving Up Music and Doing His Haunting Somewhere Else." From *Frankenstein Makes a Sandwich*, by Adam Rex. Harcourt, 2006.

This last entry of the Phantom of the Opera poems is sung to the traditional song "B-I-N-G-O." "He was never the same-o."

Short Story

"Princess Pea." From *Once Upon a Time, the End: Asleep in 60 Seconds*, by Geoffrey Kloske. Illustrated by Barry Blitt. Atheneum, 2005.

Close the program with this short, short story altered from "The Princess and the Pea." The narrator asks if there is a pea under your bed. "Then what's your excuse? Go to bed." And with that, send your audience away until the next time.

MIX AND MATCH

Additional Picture Books

Dealey, Erin. *Little Bo Peep Can't Get to Sleep*. Illustrated by Hanako Wakiyama. Atheneum, 2005.

Peep has trouble sleeping. She would count her sheep, but she doesn't know where they are. The sheep had run away earlier in the day when Little Boy Blue scared them with his horn. Peep asks several familiar nursery-rhyme characters if they've seen her sheep. The sheep wander back home, but Peep's parents prefer that she tell them in the future if her sheep go missing.

Hopkins, Jackie Mims. *The Three Armadillies Tuff*. Illustrated by S. G. Brooks. Peachtree, 2002.

Set in the southwestern United States, this version of "The Three Billy Goats Gruff" features three armadillo sisters who try to cross the highway to the new dance hall. The road is treacherous, so they take the drainpipe that runs beneath the highway. One by one, they encounter a hungry coyote who wants a "bowl of armadilly chili." The biggest armadillo sees that the coyote is a sad loner and exclaims, "How long has it been since you've had a girls' night out?" The sisters treat the coyote to a nice meal and a fun time at the dance hall.

Kimmel, Eric. *The Three Cabritos*. Illustrated by Stephen Gilpin. Marshall Cavendish, 2007.

Three musical *cabritos* (Spanish for "young goats") try to cross the bridge on the way to a fiesta across the border in Mexico. The youngest *cabrito* is confronted by the monstrous Chupacabra, a big, blue, goat-sucking vampire monster. The young goat plays his fiddle, the monster dances, and the goat is allowed to pass. The second *cabrito* plays his guitar and follows his younger brother. The last brother plays a magical accordion that makes the monster dance until it shrivels up "like a punctured balloon."

Wheeler, Lisa. *Who's Afraid of Granny Wolf?* Illustrated by Frank Ansley. Atheneum, 2004.

A young wolf invites his pig friend over to the house to meet Granny Wolf. The pig is worried that Granny Wolf is going to eat him. Her false teeth are loose, and it's hard for the youngsters to understand her. The pig thinks Granny Wolf said "I am cooking some thin pig" when actually she said "I am cooking something big." After a series of like misunderstandings, they all enjoy vegetable soup, bread, and chocolate-chip pie.

Wilcox, Leah. *Falling for Rapunzel*. Illustrated by Lydia Monks. Putnam, 2003.

The prince calls up to Rapunzel to throw down her hair. Instead, she throws down underwear. Rapunzel has problems hearing the prince. He asks for her curly locks. She throws down dirty socks. When he calls for a rope, she throws him a cantaloupe. When he tells her to throw down her braid, Rapunzel tosses her maid out the window. The prince falls in love with the maid, and they ride off.

Zalben, Jane Breskin. *Hey, Mama Goose*. Illustrated by Emilie Chollat. Dutton, 2005.

Several nursery-rhyme and folklore characters move from house to house. The old woman who lived in a shoe moves her brood to Snow White's cottage.

Snow White has already gone to live with Rapunzel. They rent a room out to Rumpelstiltskin until he moves into the gingerbread home of Hansel and Gretel. They all eventually return to their original dwellings and realize that "there's no place like home."

Additional Songs

"Big Bad Wolf." From *I Sang It Just for You,* by Mary Kaye. Mary Kaye Music, 2003.

"Goldilocks Rap." From *Teddy Bear's Greatest Hits,* by Bill Shontz. Bearspaw, 1997.

"Three Billy Goats Groove." From *Dana's Best Rock and Roll Fairy Tales,* by Dana. RMFK, 1999.

"Visiting Cinderella." From *40 Winks,* by Jessica Harper. Alacazam, 1998.

Barnyard Fun

PROGRAM AT A GLANCE

Opening Song: "Get Back, Farmer Mac" from *Grandpa's Truck* by Eric Ode
Picture Book: *Big Chickens* by Leslie Helakoski
Picture Book: *Moo Who?* by Margie Palatini
Poem: "Cows in the Kitchen" by Bruce Lansky from *Rolling in the Aisles:*
    A Collection of Laugh-Out-Loud Poems
Musical Activity: "Farmer Brown's Tractor," traditional; adapted by Rob Reid
Picture Book: *Oh, Crumps!/¡Ay, Caramba!* by Lee Bock
Poem: "Barnyard Talk" from *Squeal and Squawk: Barnyard Talk* by Susan Pearson
Picture Book: *The Noisy Farm* by Marni McGee
Song: "Old MacDonald Had a Farm," traditional

PREPARATION AND PRESENTATION

Opening Song

"Get Back, Farmer Mac." From *Grandpa's Truck,* by Eric Ode. Deep Rooted Music, 2003.

As the audience enters the story program area, play this raplike farm song. Ode has many farm-related songs on this particular recording. "Get Back, Farmer Mac" does a nice job of setting a lively mood for the program.

Picture Book

Big Chickens, by Leslie Helakoski. Illustrated by Henry Cole. Dutton, 2006.

Bad things happen to four worrywart chickens. They see a wolf and run into the woods. They fall in a ditch, bump into cows, fall off a boat, stumble into a cave, and encounter the wolf once again. The chickens "shrieked, squeaked, and freaked" and frighten the wolf. Split your audience into three groups before you share the picture book. Before each episode, one chicken states something that worries her. The other chickens say "Me too," "Me three," and "Me four." Assign one of these lines to each group and point to them as the lines appear in the book.

Picture Book

Moo Who? by Margie Palatini. Illustrated by Keith Graves. HarperCollins, 2004.

Hilda Mae Heifer loves to sing. She is struck by a cow pie and loses her moo. She tries a variety of animal noises. She honks at the goose, who immediately instructs Hilda on the characteristics of geese. Hilda goes through the same pattern with the chickens, the pig, and the cat. Finally, Hilda gets her moo back, and the other farm animals purchase earplugs. Palatini's subtle dialogue throughout the text works especially well with the adults in the audience. When the pig asks, "Are your relatives big boars?" Hilda thinks, "Well . . . yes. Maybe that did describe some members of her family."

Poem

"Cows in the Kitchen," by Bruce Lansky. From *Rolling in the Aisles: A Collection of Laugh-Out-Loud Poems,* edited by Bruce Lansky. Meadowbrook, 2004.

The adults in the audience will surely groan when they hear that the poem's narrator is surprised that the cows "made so many pies."

Musical Activity

"Farmer Brown's Tractor," traditional; adapted by Rob Reid.

I took the camp song "John Brown's Chevy" and made it a farm musical activity. This is another activity that works best when older kids and adults are around to help the younger children. Sing to the tune of "The Battle Hymn of the Republic."

> Farmer Brown's tractor had a puncture in its tire,
>
> Farmer Brown's tractor had a puncture in its tire,
>
> Farmer Brown's tractor had a puncture in its tire,
>
> And he patched it up with chewing gum.

(Repeat and substitute the word tractor *with a steering motion.)*
Farmer Brown's *(steering motion)* had a puncture in its tire,
Farmer Brown's *(steering motion)* had a puncture in its tire,
Farmer Brown's *(steering motion)* had a puncture in its tire,
And he patched it up with chewing gum.

(Sing it a third time and substitute the word puncture *with a hissing noise.)*
Farmer Brown's *(steering motion)* had a *(hiss)* in its tire,
Farmer Brown's *(steering motion)* had a *(hiss)* in its tire,
Farmer Brown's *(steering motion)* had a *(hiss)* in its tire,
And he patched it up with chewing gum.

(Sing it a fourth time and substitute the word tire *with the motion of making a circle with arms.)*
Farmer Brown's *(steering motion)* had a *(hiss)* in its *(circle motion)*,
Farmer Brown's *(steering motion)* had a *(hiss)* in its *(circle motion)*,
Farmer Brown's *(steering motion)* had a *(hiss)* in its *(circle motion)*,
And he patched it up with chewing gum.

(Sing it one last time and substitute the words chewing gum *with making a chewing noise and motion of stretching the gum.)*
Farmer Brown's *(steering motion)* had a *(hiss)* in its *(circle motion)*,
Farmer Brown's *(steering motion)* had a *(hiss)* in its *(circle motion)*,
Farmer Brown's *(steering motion)* had a *(hiss)* in its *(circle motion)*,
And he patched it up with *(make chewing motions; then mime stretching the gum in front of your mouth)*.

Picture Book

Oh, Crumps!/¡Ay, Caramba! by Lee Bock. Illustrated by Morgan Midgett. Raven Tree, 2003.

This bilingual picture book follows Farmer Felandro as he goes to bed after a busy day. He hears the goats and realizes he forgot to put them in their pens. He settles down once again but then hears the dogs barking. This pattern continues throughout the night. Once he gets one animal settled down, another makes a commotion. The kids in the audience can help make the animal noises. The adults can make a grumbling noise every time the farmer says, "Oh, crumps!" An added benefit would be to have a Spanish-speaking volunteer read the Spanish passages immediately after the English passages.

Poem

"Barnyard Talk." From *Squeal and Squawk: Barnyard Talk,* by Susan Pearson. Marshall Cavendish, 2004.

Each line of this litany of animal noises can be followed by the appropriate noise from the audience. "Hens are clucking, / Roosters crowing." The poem ends on the line, "I'm not sleeping!"

Picture Book

The Noisy Farm, by Marni McGee. Illustrated by Leonie Shearing. Bloomsbury, 2004.

The rooster begins to crow when the sun first appears, and the farm is soon filled with lots of noises. What sets this picture book apart from the many farm-animal noise books on the market are the nonanimal sound effects the audience members can make. The bedsprings "Squeak" and "Creak" when the farmer hops out of bed. When the pail bumps against the farmer's knee, it makes a "Pong, pong, poink" noise. The milk goes "Spling-splosh" into the pail, and the kitten laps it up with a "Lip-lap." The coffeepot gurgles, the frying pan sizzles, and "the porridge on top of the stove says, 'Bubble-de-blip, bubble-de-blop!'"

Song

"Old MacDonald Had a Farm," traditional.

Pamela Beall and Susan Nipp, the brains behind the Wee Sing series, added these clever motions to the traditional song on their recording *Wee Sing Children's Songs and Fingerplays* (Price Stern Sloan, 1977). Start the first verse by singing "Old MacDonald had a farm, E-I-E-I-O. And on his farm he had some chicks, E-I-E-I-O." Have everyone bob their heads like chickens. Subsequent verses find the audience members flapping their elbows for ducks, making milking motions for cows, hooking thumbs and fanning out fingers for a turkey tail, making donkey ears out of hands, and (my favorite) pushing up noses for pigs.

MIX AND MATCH

Additional Picture Books

Bruss, Deborah. *Book! Book! Book!* Illustrated by Tiphanie Beeke. Scholastic, 2001.

Author Bruss took an old library joke and turned it into a cumulative trip to the library for the farm animals. The librarian has trouble understanding the animals, but when the hen clucks, "Book! Book! Book!" the librarian hands the hen three books. The other animals are ecstatic and happy . . . all except for the bullfrog, who complains that he already "Read it." It never fails—the kids laugh at the bullfrog voice, and the adults simply groan.

Cronin, Doreen. *Duck for President.* **Illustrated by Betsy Lewin. Simon & Schuster, 2004.**

The farm animals want "a kinder, gentler farm" and elect Duck to lead the farm. All of the Cronin-Lewin farm picture books are excellent story program resources. *Duck for President* particularly layers the humor that appeals to both kids and adults. "He even played saxophone on late-night television."

The other picture books in this series that work best for family story programs include

> *Click, Clack, Moo: Cows That Type.* Simon & Schuster, 2000.
> *Dooby Dooby Moo.* Simon & Schuster, 2006.
> *Giggle, Giggle, Quack.* Simon & Schuster, 2002.

Krosoczka, Jarrett J. *Punk Farm.* **Knopf, 2005.**

The coolest band on the farm is composed of a sheep on lead vocals, a cow on drums, a goat on bass guitar, a pig on lead guitar, and a chicken on keyboards. When Farmer Joe goes to bed, the band puts on a concert for the other animals. The sheep asks, "Who's ready to rock?" and launches into a loud version of "Old MacDonald." Have fun belting out the sheep's final line: "EEEE-I-EEE-I-YEEEEEEOOOOOOOOWWWWWW! OW! OW! Thank you, Wisconsin!"

Lawrence, John. *This Little Chick.* **Candlewick, 2002.**

The little chick is able to imitate the sounds of the other animals. He oinks when he plays with the pigs, quacks along with the ducks, and also makes the sounds of the cows, frogs, and sheep. When he's with his mother, he doesn't just cheep. He mixes in all of the animal noises. The book ends with a little mouse squeak.

Palatini, Margie. *The Web Files.* **Illustrated by Richard Egielski. Hyperion, 2001.**

Palatini combines nursery-rhyme characters with the old television show *Dragnet* in this mystery set on a farm. Someone stole the hen's peppers. After careful investigation, Ducktective Web accuses That Dirty Rat. The text is loaded with pop-culture references that will especially delight the adults. "You say to-may-toes . . . I say to-mah-toes . . . Somebody just hauled the whole thing off!"

Tekavec, Heather. *What's That Awful Smell?* **Illustrated by Margaret Spengler. Dial, 2004.**

Dog runs to the barn but stops short when he smells something awful. The other farm animals join him and discover a little piglet. They try to cover it with hay to get rid of its smell. They next try to push it in a puddle, spread flowers over the piglet, place the pig in the chicken coop, and spread berries on the piglet's back. "But the smell didn't go away." Finally, the cat shows up and uncovers his lunch from the barn—a smelly liver, onion, and tuna-fish sandwich.

Additional Songs

"Barnyard Boogie." From *Sing-a-Move-a-Dance,* by Colleen and Uncle Squaty. Colleen and Uncle Squaty, 2005.

"Cows in the Kitchen." From *Little Ears: Songs for Reading Readiness,* by Fran Avni. Leapfrog School House, 2000.

"Down by the Barnyard." From *Sing It! Say It! Stamp It! Sway It!* vol. 3, by Peter and Ellen Allard. 80-Z Music, 2002.

"Goofy Old MacDonald." From *H.U.M.—All Year Long,* by Carole Peterson. Macaroni Soup, 2003.

"New Chicken Dance." From *La Di Da La Di Di Dance with Me,* by the Learning Station. Monopoli/Learning Station, 2004.

"Welcome to the Farm." From *Grandpa's Truck,* by Eric Ode. Deep Rooted Music, 2003.

Big and Gray

PROGRAM AT A GLANCE

Opening Song: "Elephant Hide and Seek" from *Marvelous Day* by SteveSongs
Picture Book: *Hippo! No, Rhino* by Jeff Newman
Picture Book: *My Friend Is Sad* by Mo Willems
Movement Activity: "An Elephant Came to Play, Play, Play" by Rob Reid
Picture Book/Felt Board: *I've Got an Elephant* by Anne Ginkel
Poem: "The Elephant" from *Hippopotamus Stew, and Other Silly Animal Poems*
    by Joan Horton
Picture Book: *Hilda Must Be Dancing* by Karma Wilson
Movement Activity: "The Hippo Chant," traditional
Picture Book: *Kiss Kiss!* by Margaret Wild

PREPARATION AND PRESENTATION

Opening Song

"Elephant Hide and Seek." From *Marvelous Day*, by SteveSongs. Rounder Records, 2006.

Play this lively song as audience members enter the story program area. Steve Roslonek, aka SteveSongs, sings about the difficulties elephants have playing the popular game of hide-and-seek because parts of them inevitably stick out.

Picture Book

Hippo! No, Rhino, **by Jeff Newman. Little, Brown, 2006.**

Rhino is upset because Randy the zookeeper put up the Hippo sign in front of his exhibit. Folks come by to look at the hippo, which makes Rhino holler, "No, Rhino!" He pleads for someone to "Fix the Sign-O!" Rhino's voice is sparse but fun to read aloud. Finally, a little boy hears Rhino and fixes the sign. However, Randy is at it again. At the hippo exhibit, he puts up the sign for Porcupine-O.

Picture Book

My Friend Is Sad, **by Mo Willems. Hyperion, 2007.**

Elephant is sad, and Piggie tries to cheer him up. Piggie first dresses up like a cowboy, then a clown, and finally a robot. But Elephant remains sad. When Piggie shows up as Piggie, Elephant is delighted because his friend is back. He tells Piggie that "my best friend was not there" to see the cowboy, clown, and robot. Piggie ends the book by stating, "You need new glasses." Check out the other books in the Elephant and Piggie series by Mo Willems.

Movement Activity

"An Elephant Came to Play, Play, Play," by Rob Reid.

Have everyone stand for this call-and-response chant. Instruct them to make a trunk with one arm on the word *elephant,* make a horn with one hand on the word *rhino,* and hold both arms in front of their faces to form a mouth on the word *hippo.* Next, they should hold their hands overhead on the word *big* and place their hands in front of their tummies on *fat.* Finally, they should shake their "hipp-os" on the lines, *play, play, play* and *gray, gray, gray.*

>An elephant came to play, play, play,   (An elephant came to play, play, play,)
>He's big and fat and gray, gray, gray.   (He's big and fat and gray, gray, gray.)
>
>A rhino came to play, play, play,   (A rhino came to play, play, play,)
>She's big and fat and gray, gray, gray.   (She's big and fat and gray, gray, gray.)
>
>A hippo came to play, play, play,   (A hippo came to play, play, play,)
>He's big and fat and gray, gray, gray.   (He's big and fat and gray, gray, gray.)
>
>*(Tell everyone to pick one of the three animals and make the hand gestures for it for the final verse.)*

All three came by to play, play, play,   (All three came by to play, play, play,)
They're big and fat and gray, gray, gray.   (They're big and fat and gray, gray, gray.)

Picture Book/Felt Board

I've Got an Elephant, **by Anne Ginkel. Illustrated by Janie Bynum. Peachtree, 2006.**

Make ten felt elephants and one felt monkey. Patterns can be found on the Internet by typing "Coloring Pages" on any search engine. Place the characters on a felt board one at a time as the story progresses. A little girl has one elephant that sleeps in her bed. When she goes to school, however, the elephant goes out and finds a new friend. The girl now has two elephants. When she goes shopping, the elephants find another friend and so on until the girl has ten elephants, and she hollers "Enough!" She packs all ten elephants off to the zoo but visits them every Sunday. She starts all over again by making friends with one monkey.

Poem

"The Elephant." From *Hippopotamus Stew, and Other Silly Animal Poems,* **by Joan Horton. Holt, 2006.**

The narrator wonders, how many tissues does an "elephant need for a sniffly nose"? Could it be a boxful, a trainload, or a trunkful?

Picture Book

Hilda Must Be Dancing, **by Karma Wilson. Illustrated by Suzanne Watts. McElderry, 2004.**

Hilda the hippo loves to dance. Unfortunately, she makes the jungle floor "shake and quake." The other animals shout, "Hilda must be dancing!" Teach the audience to shout this refrain. Hilda dances ballet, the tango, square dance, the flamenco, the rumba, the samba, and disco. Finally, she discovers that water ballet doesn't shake the jungle floor.

Movement Activity

"The Hippo Chant," traditional.

This call-and-response chant is featured a lot as a silly camp activity. On the words *What can,* have audience members shrug their left shoulders. On the words *make a,* have them shrug their right shoulders, and on the word *hippo,* have them shrug both shoulders. On the word *smile,* have them lean forward and make an arc or a smile with their heads and upper bodies. Practice this a few times, and they'll pick it up quickly. They'll repeat the same motions for the second line, "What can make him run a mile?" They'll also pick up the other motions on the call-and-response part.

> What can make a hippo smile?   (What can make a hippo smile?)
> What can make him run a mile?   (What can make him run a mile?)
> It's not a party with a paper hat.   (It's not a party with a paper hat.)
> *(Make a triangle with hands over head.)*
>
> Nor a bag of candy that will make him fat.   (Nor a bag of candy that will make him fat.)
> *(Place arms in front of tummy.)*
>
> That's not what hippos do.   (That's not what hippos do.)
> *(Wag finger and shake head.)*
> They ooze through the gooze without any shoes.   (They ooze through the gooze without any shoes.)
> *(Shimmy.)*
> They wade through the water till their lips turn blue.   (They wade through the water till their lips turn blue.)
> *(Make swimming motions.)*
> That's what hippos do.   (That's what hippos do.)
> *(Nod yes.)*
>
> What can make a hippo smile?   (What can make a hippo smile?)
> What can make him run a mile?   (What can make him run a mile?)
> It's not a tune on the old violin.   (It's not a tune on the old violin.)
> *(Play imaginary violin.)*
> Or listening to the whistling wind.   (Or listening to the whistling wind.)
> *(Cup ears and whistle.)*
>
> That's not what hippos do.   (That's not what hippos do.)
> *(Wag finger and shake head.)*
> They ooze through the gooze without any shoes.   (They ooze through the gooze without any shoes.)
> *(Shimmy.)*

They wade through the water till their lips turn blue.   (They wade
through the water till their lips turn blue.)

(Make swimming motions.)

That's what hippos do.   (That's what hippos do.)

(Nod yes.)

Picture Book

Kiss Kiss! **by Margaret Wild. Simon & Schuster, 2003.**

Baby Hippo is in such a rush to play that he forgets to kiss his mama. He sees the elephants kiss, as well as the rhinos, the lions, the zebras, and the monkeys. He rushes back to kiss his mother, but she's nowhere to be seen. "Then out of the deep, deep water appeared two eyes." Mama says "Peekaboo," and, of course, they kiss.

MIX AND MATCH

Additional Picture Books

Howard, Arthur. *The Hubbub Above.* Harcourt, 2005.

A little girl lives on the fifty-second floor of a city high-rise. "'It's heavenly here,' Sydney thought." However, the Kabooms—a family of elephants—move in upstairs. "They walked loud. They talked loud . . . they cha-cha-ed very, VERY loud." Sydney complains but soon joins the party.

Lester, Helen. *Hurty Feelings.* Illustrated by Lynn Munsinger. Houghton Mifflin. 2004.

Fragility is a hippo whose feelings get the best of her. She exaggerates comments by others out of proportion, weeps, and wails: "You hurt my feeeeelings." She does, however, stand up to Rudy the rude elephant. He stops his bullying and cries out "You hurt me feeeeelings!"

Magoon, Scott. *Hugo and Miles in I've Painted Everything.* Houghton Mifflin, 2007.

Hugo the elephant is a painter who runs out of things to paint. His friend Miles, a dog, takes Hugo to Paris and shows him different perspectives and painting styles. They head back home, where Hugo paints with renewed gusto.

Murray, Marjorie Dennis. *Hippo Goes Bananas!* Illustrated by Kevin O'Malley. Marshall Cavendish, 2006.

Hippo wakes up with a toothache, but the other jungle animals believe Hippo is going bananas. They spread rumors about Hippo knocking down trees, kicking them off the cliff, damming up the water, and flooding the Serengeti. The animals push Hippo into the water, and as he tumbles, his bad tooth pops out. Unfortunately, he now has a headache.

Payne, Tony, and Jan Payne. *The Hippo-Not-Amus.* **Illustrated by Guy Parker-Rees. Orchard, 2003.**

Portly is bored being a hippo. He gives a try at being a rhino. He fashions two pieces of wood into rhino horns, but they stick "out just anywhere." He also tries to be a bat, an elephant, and a giraffe. He returns home as a "hippo-gir-ele-bat-onoceros." (Practice saying this word aloud in advance!) Of course, he learns that he'd rather be a hippo.

Schwartz, Amy. *Starring Miss Darlene.* **Roaring Brook, 2007.**

Darlene the hippo loves theater. She gets the part of the Flood in a production of *Noah's Ark.* Darlene is supposed to throw a pan of water onstage, but she trips and gets the local theater critic wet. His review the next day praises the show for its "audience participation." Two more plays, two more mishaps from Darlene, and two more surprisingly glowing reviews round out this book.

Additional Songs

"Elephant Train." From *Wiggles, Jiggles, and Giggles,* by Stephen Fite. Melody House, 2000.

"Hey, Hippopotamus." From *Yellow Bus,* by Justin Roberts. Justin Roberts, 2001.

"The Hippopotamus Song." From *I Love My Shoes,* by Eric Ode. Deep Rooted Music, 2003.

"Our Imaginary Rhino." From *Meltdown!* by Justin Roberts. Justin Roberts, 2006.

"Rhino." From *The Lost Songs of Kenland,* by Ken Lonnquist. Kenland, 1998.

"Zousan (Little Elephant)." From *You Are My Little Bird,* by Elizabeth Mitchell. Smithsonian Folkways, 2006.

Birdland

PROGRAM AT A GLANCE

Opening Song: "Little Bird, Little Bird" from *You Are My Little Bird* by Elizabeth Mitchell

Picture Book: *Franny B. Kranny, There's a Bird in Your Hair!* by Harriet Lerner and Susan Goldhor

Creative Dramatics: "Be a Bird"

Picture Book: *Duck and Goose* by Tad Hills

Song: "The More We Tweet Together," traditional; adapted by Rob Reid

Picture Book/Felt Board: *There Is a Bird on Your Head!* by Mo Willems

Picture Book: *Cheep! Cheep!* by Julie Stiegemeyer

Musical Activity: "Mother Gooney Bird," traditional

Picture Book/Movement Activity: *Five Little Chicks* by Nancy Tafuri

Picture Book: *Bird Songs* by Betsy Franco

PREPARATION AND PRESENTATION

Opening Song

"Little Bird, Little Bird." From *You Are My Little Bird*, by Elizabeth Mitchell. Smithsonian Folkways, 2006.

Elizabeth Mitchell has a beautiful, mesmerizing voice that will capture the attention of audience members as they enter the program area. Here, she solicits bird suggestions from children, who join her in singing on the recording.

Picture Book

Franny B. Kranny, There's a Bird in Your Hair! by Harriet Lerner and Susan Goldhor. Illustrated by Helen Oxenbury. HarperCollins, 2001.

Franny's long, frizzy hair gets caught in things, makes another kid sneeze, and is constantly tangled. A hairdresser piles her hair "in a giant heap." A bird lands on top of Franny's hair and snuggles down. Franny likes the bird and lets it stay. After everyone in the family accepts this strange phenomenon, Franny decides to cut her hair. "A little birdie told me to."

Creative Dramatics

"Be a Bird"

Direct the audience members to stand and pretend they are birds. Ask them to play follow the leader as if the leader were a bird. Ask them to flap their wings, slurp worms, fly around the room, and sing.

Picture Book

Duck and Goose, by Tad Hills. Schwartz & Wade, 2006.

Duck and Goose hilariously mistake a ball for an egg. They each claim it. Duck states he saw it first. Goose counters by touching it first. They decide to keep the "egg" warm and sit side by side on top of the ball. Together, they make plans for the little chick once it hatches. A blue bird arrives and asks if it can play with the ball. Duck and Goose are surprised to learn that it is not an egg and then play games with the ball.

Song

"The More We Tweet Together," traditional; adapted by Rob Reid.

Sing this bird version to the tune of the traditional song "The More We Get Together." Ask the audience members to pretend they are a choir of birds and sing along. The flapping of wings is optional.

> The more we tweet together, together, together,
>
> The more we tweet together, the happier we'll be.
>
> For your friends are my friends, and my friends are your friends,
>
> The more we tweet together, the happier we'll be.
>
> Tweet, tweet, tweet, tweet.
>
> The more we hoot together, together, together,
>
> The more we hoot together, the happier we'll be.

For your friends are my friends, and my friends are your friends,

The more we hoot together, the happier we'll be.

Hoot, hoot, hoot, hoot.

The more we caw together, together, together,

The more we caw together, the happier we'll be.

For your friends are my friends, and my friends are your friends,

The more we caw together, the happier we'll be.

Caw, caw, caw, caw.

Ask audience members to suggest other birdcalls for additional verses.

Picture Book/Felt Board

There Is a Bird on Your Head! **by Mo Willems. Hyperion, 2007.**

A bird lands on Elephant's head. A second bird joins the first. Pig informs his friend Elephant that the birds are lovebirds and they are making a nest. Soon, there are three eggs in the nest on Elephant's head. Of course, the eggs hatch. Elephant angrily declares that he does not want "three baby chicks, two birds, and a nest on my head!" He politely asks the birds to leave and they do—onto Piggie's head. This is a fun book to simply read aloud while showing the pictures or to read it and manipulate felt versions of the characters.

Picture Book

Cheep! Cheep! **by Julie Stiegemeyer. Illustrated by Carol Baicker-McKee. Bloomsbury, 2006.**

Three birds sitting on a perch wait for an egg to hatch. They start out sleeping. When they hear a peep, they quietly creep, leap, and land in a heap. They welcome the new chick and go back to sleep. The verso of each page contains one word, such as *cheep*. Most of the recto pages repeat the word three times. You can read the first word and let the audience repeat it three times to match the picture book text. The room will soon be filled with "cheeps" and "peeps."

Musical Activity

"Mother Gooney Bird," traditional.

Ask everyone to stand for this fun camp activity. Sing to the tune of "Father Abraham."

Mother Gooney Bird had many chicks,

Many chicks had Mother Gooney Bird.

They didn't laugh,
They didn't cry,
All they could do was go like this:
Left wing!   (*move left arm*)

Mother Gooney Bird had many chicks,
Many chicks had Mother Gooney Bird.
They didn't laugh,
They didn't cry,
All they could do was go like this:
Left wing!   (*move left arm*)
Right wing!   (*move right arm*)

Mother Gooney Bird had many chicks,
Many chicks had Mother Gooney Bird.
They didn't laugh,
They didn't cry,
All they could do was go like this:
Left wing!   (*move left arm*)
Right wing!   (*move right arm*)
Left leg!   (*move left leg*)

Mother Gooney Bird had many chicks,
Many chicks had Mother Gooney Bird.
They didn't laugh,
They didn't cry,
All they could do was go like this:
Left wing!   (*move left arm*)
Right wing!   (*move right arm*)
Left leg!   (*move left leg, hop on right*)
Tail feather!   (*sit*)

Picture Book/Movement Activity

Five Little Chicks, **by Nancy Tafuri. Simon & Schuster, 2006.**

The chicks are hungry and find different things to eat. Ask everyone to stand and hold up their hands. Hold up one finger for each chick as they hatch. Wiggle a different finger as each chick runs off. Have the audience repeat the repetitive line,

"Peep! What can I eat?" Mama Hen has the chicks run to the patch where they scratch. Scratch with the hens. The chicks finally snuggle and sleep.

Picture Book

Bird Songs, by Betsy Franco. Illustrated by Steve Jenkins. McElderry, 2007.

This sound-effects book is also a backward counting book. A woodpecker makes ten "tat tat" sounds in the front yard. This is followed by nine "coos" of mourning doves on the telephone wire. Encourage the audience to make the bird sounds, including those of the sparrow, gull, chickadee, mallard duck, crow, robin, thrasher, and hummingbird. When the sun goes down, a mockingbird "copies all of the songs and calls she has heard during the day," ending the story and the program with a cacophony of noise.

MIX AND MATCH

Additional Picture Books

Dunrea, Olivier. *Ollie.* Houghton Mifflin, 2003.

Ollie is inside his egg, and he won't come out. "Gossie and Gertie have been waiting for weeks." He moves the egg around and around, but he still won't come out. Gossie and Gertie finally say, "Don't come out." That does it. Parents especially will enjoy Ollie's stubborn attitude.

Freedman, Claire. *Gooseberry Goose.* Illustrated by Vanessa Cabban. Tiger Tales, 2003.

Gooseberry is learning how to fly. He wants to show Beaver how good he is with takeoffs and landings, but Beaver is too busy preparing for winter. He also wants to show off his new flying talents to Squirrel, Mouse, and Rabbit, but they, too, are hard at work getting ready for the cold season. Gooseberry is worried that he and his parents aren't doing anything to get ready for winter. His parents assure him that geese fly south for the winter and that his flying practice was his way of getting ready.

Harrison, David L. *Dylan, the Eagle-Hearted Chicken.* Illustrated by Karen Stormer Brooks. Boyds Mill, 2002.

A crow steals the young chicken Dylan while he's still in his egg. The crow drops the egg into an eagle's nest to get away from Dylan's mother. The eagle mother raises Dylan as her own child. Dylan communicates with his real mother, who is down below on the ground. At the same time, Dylan is wary of his eagle siblings. They think he looks good to eat. A fox heads for the hen house. Dylan courageously leaps from the eagle's nest and saves the day.

Horowitz, Dave. *Beware of Tigers.* **Putnam, 2006.**

This silly book features two birds having a good time sitting on a curb with a can of Herb's Gourmet Worms. A third bird comes along and warns the two that a tiger is coming. The two birds laugh until a tiger arrives on a city bus. The tiger tells the birds not to worry and sings and dances for them. The tiger then smiles and opens his mouth. The birds fly away just in time and find an ally in a crocodile.

Keller, Holly. *Sophie's Window.* **Greenwillow, 2005.**

Caruso is a pigeon who is afraid to fly. A gust of wind carries him to a window where he meets Sophie, a dog. Sophie tries to lead Caruso back to his home—the "yellow building with a small shed on its top." Caruso has trouble keeping up, so the little bird hops on Sophie's back, up the building's elevator, and back to Mama and Papa pigeon. Days later, Caruso learns to fly. His first visit is to see Sophie.

Tankard, Jeremy. *Grumpy Bird.* **Scholastic, 2007.**

Bird is too grumpy to fly, so he walks. Sheep decides to join Bird on the walk. Soon, they are joined by Rabbit, Raccoon, Beaver, and Fox. Bird's grumpy dialogue will amuse the grown-ups in the audience. Bird starts leading the group in a game of follow the leader, and his mood improves. They all fly back to his nest—yes, the mammals fly, too.

Additional Songs

"Caw Caw Caw." From *Magic Parade*, by Elizabeth McMahon. Mrs. McPuppet, 2006.

"Night Owl." From *Night Time!* by Dan Zanes. Festival Five Records, 2002.

"Pink Floyd Saves Hugh Manatee." From *Eat Every Bean and Pea on Your Plate*, by Daddy A Go Go. Boyd's Tone, 2006.

"The Puffin Song." From *Don't Kiss a Codfish/When I Grow Up*, by Tom Knight. Tom Knight, 2005.

"Soaring Eagle." From *Wiggles, Jiggles, and Giggles*, by Stephen Fite. Melody House, 2000.

"Wild Bird Round." From *Earthy Songs*, by Ken Lonnquist. Kenland, 2006.

Black Bears, Brown Bears, Polar, Panda, and Teddy Bears

PROGRAM AT A GLANCE

Opening Song: "Freddy Bear the Teddy Bear" from *Ralph's World* by Ralph's World

Picture Book: *Milo's Hat Trick* by Jon Agee

Movement Activity: "Five Bear Cubs," traditional

Picture Book: *Zen Shorts* by Jon J. Muth

Musical Activity: "Baby Bear Roars" by Rob Reid

Picture Book: *Goldilocks Returns* by Lisa Campbell Ernst

Movement Activity: "Five Little Teddy Bears Jumping on the Bed," traditional; adapted by Rob Reid

Picture Book: *The Three Snow Bears* by Jan Brett

Movement Activity: "Looking for Polar Bears," adapted by Rob Reid

Picture Book: *Orange Pear Apple Bear* by Emily Gravett

PREPARATION AND PRESENTATION

Opening Song

"Freddy Bear the Teddy Bear." From *Ralph's World*, by Ralph's World. Mini Fresh, 2001.

Freddy Bear the Teddy Bear wants to dance and sing with his friends at a hootenanny, perfect for a family storytime setting. Ralph Covert, another former rock star now making music for kids, worked with the Old Town School of Folk Music before becoming a solo children's artist.

Picture Book

Milo's Hat Trick, **by Jon Agee. Hyperion, 2001.**

Milo the Magnificent is a pathetic magician. He is told to pull a rabbit out of his hat or else. Instead of a rabbit, Milo catches a bear. The bear is very adept at hiding in a hat. He agrees to help Milo with his show, but the two become separated. The bear finally locates Milo, and the magician becomes a success. "After popping in and out of seven hundred and sixty-two hats," the bear decides to quit the show. Milo lets him go and learns how to dive into the hat himself. The illustration of the bear popping out of the hat in a crowded restaurant going "TA-DA!" is precious.

Movement Activity

"Five Bear Cubs," traditional.

> Five bear cubs were peeking from their cave.   *(hold up both hands, left hand horizontal; hide right fist behind left hand)*
>
> The first one said, "C'mon, we're brave!"   *(hold up thumb on the right hand, which is "peeking" over the top of the left hand)*
>
> The second one said, "Let's see what's outside!"   *(add pointer finger)*
>
> The third one said, "I'd rather stay and hide!"   *(add middle finger)*
>
> The fourth one said, "Our mama will be real mad!"   *(add ring finger)*
>
> The fifth one said, "Nah, she'll be proud and glad!"   *(add pinkie finger)*
>
> Then "GRRRR" went Mama Bear, seeing her cubs outside.
>
> And the five bear cubs scrambled back inside.   *(wiggle all five fingers and then hide them once again behind left hand)*

Picture Book

Zen Shorts, **by Jon J. Muth. Scholastic, 2005.**

A large panda named Stillwater moves near three children. He tells each of them a different short story that imparts Zen wisdom. The children in your audience will enjoy the simple plots, while older children and adults will take deeper meanings from the stories. My favorite story is about a monk who carries a woman across water. She leaves without thanking him. The monk's companion is angry that the woman didn't thank the monk. The monk replies that he set the woman down hours ago. "Why are *you* still carrying her?"

Musical Activity

"Baby Bear Roars," by Rob Reid.

When advertising the program, notify audience members to bring along teddy bears. Have extras in the story program area. Sing the following to the tune of "Mary Had a Little Lamb." Say the first verse in a quiet voice and the second verse in a loud voice.

> Baby bears make quiet roars, quiet roars, quiet roars.
>
> Baby bears make quiet roars.
>
> Let's hear your bear cub roar!   *(have participants hold up their teddy bears and roar quietly)*
>
> But when they grow, they roar real loud, roar real loud, roar real loud.
>
> When they grow, they roar real loud.
>
> Let's hear you roar real loud.   *(have participants hold up their teddy bears and roar loudly)*

Picture Book

Goldilocks Returns, **by Lisa Campbell Ernst. Simon & Schuster, 2000.**

Goldilocks is an old locksmith who has guilty memories about her past behavior toward the bears. Baby Bear is now fifty years old (and still called Baby Bear). The three bears are out for a walk when Goldi arrives. She installs several locks and bolts on the bears' door. She stocks their cabinets with health food. She refurbishes their chairs and beds. Exhausted by her labor, she falls asleep on Baby Bear's bed. The bears notice the changes and find "Someone's been sleeping in my bed, and here she is—AGAIN!" The bears are not comfortable with the new changes, but a new and funny opportunity shows up in the end.

Movement Activity

"Five Little Teddy Bears Jumping on the Bed," traditional; adapted by Rob Reid.

This is the exact same rhyme as the traditional "Five Little Monkeys Jumping on the Bed" with teddy bears substituting for monkeys and *I* for *Mama*. Ask the audience to hold up five fingers on one hand and have that hand "jump" up and down on the other hand on the first line of each verse. Hold head in hands for the second line. Mime calling on the phone for the third line. Shake finger on the fourth line. An alternative is to have the children bounce their teddy bears up and down.

Five little teddy bears jumping on the bed.   *(hold up five fingers)*
One fell off and hurt its head.
I called the doctor and the doctor said,
"No more teddy bears jumping on the bed!"

Four little teddy bears jumping on the bed.   *(hold up four fingers)*
One fell off and hurt its head.
I called the doctor and the doctor said,
"No more teddy bears jumping on the bed!"

Three little teddy bears jumping on the bed.   *(hold up three fingers)*
One fell off and hurt its head.
I called the doctor and the doctor said,
"No more teddy bears jumping on the bed!"

Two little teddy bears jumping on the bed.   *(hold up two fingers)*
One fell off and hurt its head.
I called the doctor and the doctor said,
"No more teddy bears jumping on the bed!"

One little teddy bear jumping on the bed.   *(hold up one finger)*
One fell off and hurt its head.
I called the doctor and the doctor said,
"No more teddy bears jumping on the bed!"

No more teddy bears jumping on the bed.   *(hold up fist)*
None fell off and hurt their head.
I called the doctor and the doctor said,
"Put all of your teddy bears back in your bed!"

Picture Book

The Three Snow Bears, by Jan Brett. Putnam, 2007.

Young Aloo-ki loses her team of dogs on an ice floe in this retelling of "Goldilocks and the Three Bears." She finds herself exploring an igloo. It belongs to a family of polar bears who are out for a stroll while their soup cools. The bears see Aloo-ki's dogs and rescue them. In the meantime, Aloo-ki is eating the bears' food, trying on their boots, and sleeping in their fur-covered beds. When the bears find her, Aloo-ki runs away. She finds her dogs and is astute enough to wave her thanks to the bear family.

Movement Activity

"Looking for Polar Bears," adapted by Rob Reid.

This activity is patterned after that touchstone library story program activity "We're Going on a Bear Hunt." Have the audience spread their fingers to simulate snowshoes and slap them on their legs.

> We're looking for polar bears.
> We're going to find a big one.
> We're not afraid.
> Are you? I'm not!
> We need to put on our snowshoes.   *(mime putting on snowshoes)*
> Let's go.
>
> We're looking for polar bears.
> We're going to find a big one.
> We're not afraid.
> Are you? I'm not!
>
> Here's a little hill.
> Can't go under it,
> Can't go around it.
> We'll have to climb over it.
> Careful, it's slippery!   *(slap slower as if climbing was an effort; huff and puff)*
>
> We're looking for polar bears.
> We're going to find a big one.
> We're not afraid.
> Are you? I'm not!
>
> We're at the top of the hill.
> We have to get down there.   *(point)*
> We'll have to slide.   *(move body side to side and shout "Wheeee!")*
>
> We're looking for polar bears.
> We're going to find a big one.

We're not afraid.
Are you? I'm not!

Here's some open water.
Can't go under it.
Can't go around it.
We'll have to go on top of it.
Here's a kayak!   *(mime kayak paddle motions)*
Paddle, paddle, paddle, paddle.
Finally! Here's land!   *(slap legs again)*

We're looking for polar bears.
We're going to find a big one.
We're not afraid.
Are you? I'm not!

Uh-oh! Snowstorm!
It's hard to see!   *(squint and put hands near eyes)*
Here's shelter!
It's a snow den.
Let's crawl in.   *(move hands back and forth on legs)*
Whew! That was close.
I think there's something in here with us.
I feel something furry! Is it your coat?
I see two eyes. Are they yours?
I see big teeth. They're too big for you!
It's a polar bear! Run!   *(slap hands quickly)*
Into the kayak!   *(mime kayak paddle motions)*
We're on the other side!   *(slap hands on legs)*
Climb the hill!   *(slap slower; huff and puff)*
Slide down the other side.   *(move side to side and shout "Wheeee!")*
Whew! We're safe!   *(stop)*
We can take off our snowshoes.   *(mime taking off snowshoes)*
I wasn't afraid. Were you?

Picture Book

Orange Pear Apple Bear, by Emily Gravett. Simon & Schuster, 2007.

The brief text makes a fun call-and-response experience as the audience looks at the pictures. We see an orange on the first page, a pear on the second, an apple on the third, and a brown bear on the fourth page. The four items start interacting. We see an orange-colored bear, an apple bear, and a pear bear. The bear balances and juggles the fruit before eating them. "There!"

MIX AND MATCH

Additional Picture Books

Catchpool, Michael. *Where There's a Bear, There's Trouble!* Illustrated by Vanessa Cabban. Tiger Tales, 2002.

A bear sees a bee and figures there's honey in his near future. The bee thinks, "Where there's a bear, there's trouble" and takes off. Two geese spot the bear following the bee. They think that where there's a bear, there must be berries and join the procession. Three mice see the geese and wonder if the geese will lead them to corn. One hundred bees buzz out of a hive and scatter the other animals. The audience can make the buzzing sounds of the bees, the growls of the bear, the honks of the geese, and the squeaks of the mice.

Gliori, Debi. *Mr. Bear's Vacation.* Orchard, 2000.

Mr. Bear decides it's time for the family to go on a vacation. They pack up and go hiking. They set up their tent when night begins to arrive, but things start going wrong. The tent has holes, and the poles are bent. The supper is burned. They forgot to pack the sleeping bags, and they think they see a monster (it's a cow). They head for home and decide "we all need *another* vacation to recover from our vacation." Many adults will sympathize with that sentiment.

Hayes, Karel. *The Winter Visitors.* Down East Books, 2007.

The nearly wordless format and tiny details of this book might be difficult to share with a large audience. Small groups, however, will enjoy reading about some bears that move into a cottage for the winter. The bears romp on the bed, go fishing and sledding, invite other animals in the cottage, have a party, and then rest. They wake and clean up just in time before the human summer visitors arrive.

Mason, Jane B. *Stella and the Berry Thief.* Illustrated by Loek Koopmans. Marshall Cavendish, 2004.

Stella is a young woman who keeps to herself in the country. She grows raspberries and makes prizewinning pies and preserves. One year, she finds a thief stealing her berries. She discovers that the thief is a bear. She tries everything to drive the bear away but fails. With her berries gone, Stella follows the bear into the woods. She discovers "the biggest raspberry patch Stella had ever seen." Adults will appreciate that Stella names the bear Bernie after her thieving brother-in-law.

Stein, David Ezra. *Leaves*. Putnam, 2007.

A young bear is enjoying his first year. He sees a leaf fall and asks, "Are you okay?" More and more leaves fall. The bear grows sleepy, finds a hole, and fills it with leaves. Winter arrives. We don't see the bear. He emerges in the spring and is thrilled to see that the trees have little buds.

Additional Songs

"Bear Hunt." From *On a Flying Guitar*, by SteveSongs. SteveSongs, 2000.

"Goldilocks and the 3 Bears." From *Literacy in Motion*, by the Learning Station. Monopoli/Learning Station, 2005.

"The Goldilocks Rock." From *Dana's Best Rock and Roll Fairy Tales*, by Dana. RMFK, 1999.

"My Teddy Bear." From *Again*, by Brian Kinder. Brian Kinder, 2003.

"The Teddy Bear Song." From *Fun and Games*, by Greg and Steve. Youngheart Records, 2002.

"There's a Bear in There." From *Trash Can*, by Eric Ode. Deep Rooted Music, 2002.

Bubbly Bubble Bathtime

PROGRAM AT A GLANCE

Opening Song: "Bathtub Soup" from *I Found It!* by Brady Rymer
Picture Book: *Dirt Boy* by Erik Jon Slangerup
Picture Book: *One Smart Goose* by Caroline Jayne Church
Movement Activity: "Five Little Kiddos" by Rob Reid
Picture Book: *Tub Toys* by Terry Miller Shannon and Timothy Warner
Memory Game: "Tub Toys," adapted by Rob Reid
Picture Book: *Jess and the Stinky Cowboys* by Janice Lee Smith
Picture Book: *I'm Dirty!* by Kate McMullan
Musical Activity: "This Is the Way We Take a Bath," traditional; adapted by Rob Reid

PREPARATION AND PRESENTATION

Opening Song

"Bathtub Soup." From *I Found It!* by Brady Rymer. Bumblin' Bee, 2004.

As folks enter the story program area, they'll soon find themselves singing the catchy chorus: "Bathtub soup / Bathtub soup / I want to make / Bathtub soup." Former rock musician Brady Rymer sings in a laid-back manner about all of the toys that go into the tub to make bathtub soup.

Picture Book

***Dirt Boy,* by Erik Jon Slangerup. Illustrated by John Manders. Whitman, 2000.**

Fister Farnello loves dirt, but he hates baths. He runs into the woods and encounters Dirt Man, a giant who hasn't had a bath in a thousand years. The two become friends. Fister becomes dirtier and dirtier, growing mushrooms between his toes and spewing "a thick green cloud of stink" from his mouth. Fister runs back home to his mother. "It took twenty-three bars of soap, sixteen bottles of shampoo, one hundred and seventy-nine gallons of bathwater, forty-four million bubbles, and eleven tubes of toothpaste to finally get Fister Farnello clean."

Picture Book

One Smart Goose, by Caroline Jayne Church. Orchard, 2003.

One goose splashes in a muddy pond to the jeers of the other geese. When the fox attacks the geese, it ignores the muddy goose. That goose explains to the other geese that his muddy feathers blend in the shadows, escaping the attention of the fox. The other geese take a muddy bath. When it starts snowing, the one goose takes a bath "until all his feathers were clean and gleaming." The fox attacks again and chases the dirty geese. The fox doesn't see the clean goose against the white snow. The goose trips the fox and saves the day.

Movement Activity

"Five Little Kiddos," by Rob Reid.

Five little kiddos   *(hold up five fingers)*
Rolling in the mud,   *(twirl hands)*
Mama picked up one dirty kid   *(grab back of shirt and yank up)*
And dumped him in the tub.   *(hold nose, take a deep breath, close eyes)*

Four little kiddos   *(hold up four fingers)*
Rolling in the mud,   *(twirl hands)*
Papa picked up one dirty kid   *(grab back of shirt and yank up)*
And dumped him in the tub.   *(hold nose, take a deep breath, close eyes)*

Three little kiddos   *(hold up three fingers)*
Rolling in the mud,   *(twirl hands)*
Mama picked up one dirty kid   *(grab back of shirt and yank up)*
And dumped her in the tub.   *(hold nose, take a deep breath, close eyes)*

Two little kiddos   *(hold up two fingers)*
Rolling in the mud,   *(twirl hands)*
Papa picked up one dirty kid   *(grab back of shirt and yank up)*
And dumped her in the tub.   *(hold nose, take a deep breath, close eyes)*

One little kiddo   *(hold up one finger)*
Rolling in the mud,   *(twirl hands)*
His parents picked him up   *(grab back of shirt and yank up)*
And dumped him in the tub.   *(hold nose, take a deep breath, close eyes)*

Five little kiddos   *(hold up five fingers)*
Splashing bathtub toys,   *(pretend to splash)*
Smiling 'cause they know they are   *(big smile)*
Squeaky-clean girls and boys!   *(rub skin and say, "Squeak-squeak")*

Picture Book

Tub Toys, **by Terry Miller Shannon and Timothy Warner. Illustrated by Lee Calderon. Tricycle, 2002.**

I remember my own kids doing this—throwing every single bath toy we owned into the tub. A little boy throws the following items into the tub: a rubber ducky, a windup frog, a beach ball, a strainer, toy trucks, an ice-cream container, empty bottles, an eggbeater, Tinkertoys, a plastic book, more animals, and five ships. Of course, there's no room for the boy.

Memory Game

"Tub Toys," adapted by Rob Reid.

Here's a bathtub version of a popular alphabet memory exercise. Start things off by stating, "I took a bath with an Ape." Point to a member of the audience and ask them to repeat what you said and to add something that begins with the letter B. For example, "I took a bath with an Ape and a Ball." Go around the room and have everyone add an item that begins with the next letter of the alphabet. If someone gets stuck either remembering what items were previously mentioned or coming up with a new item, the whole group can help out. The items can be real bath toys or bathtime objects (such as soap or washrags), or they can be completely silly, like cucumbers. Shoot for the whole alphabet. Every time I lead this exercise, the audience always bursts out in loud applause and high fives at the end.

Picture Book

Jess and the Stinky Cowboys, **by Janice Lee Smith. Illustrated by Lisa Thiesing. Dial, 2004.**

The story is lengthy, the pictures are small, but the dialogue is worth sharing this easy reader with any size crowd. Four stinky cowboys come to town. Deputy

Jess informs them, "We have a No-Stink law." The cowboys refuse to take a bath. They are arrested, but the jail soon smells worse "than a cow pie in July!" There are several attempts to clean the cowboys before Jess comes up with the proper solution. Teach the audience to shout out the cowboys' refrain: "No baths today, no baths tomorrow, no baths ever!"

Picture Book

***I'm Dirty!* by Kate McMullan. Illustrated by Jim McMullan. HarperCollins, 2006.**

An anthropomorphic backhoe loader takes a different type of bath after a busy day of work—a mud bath. It loves its work of cleaning trash, including ten "torn-up truck tires," nine "fractured fans," all the way down to one "wonky washing machine." It makes a lot of noise that the audience members can help make. "CLANK! BANG! RATTLE! CLUNK!" At the end of the book, the backhoe loader is very proud of being dirty.

Musical Activity

"This Is the Way We Take a Bath," traditional; adapted by Rob Reid.

Have everyone stand and act out the motions and sing this song to the tune of "Mulberry Bush."

> This is the way we fill the tub, fill the tub, fill the tub,
> This is the way we fill the tub so early in the morning.   *(mime turning on faucets)*
>
> This is the way we test the water, test the water, test the water,
> This is the way we test the water so early in the morning.   *(point toe to floor)*
>
> This is the way we wash our hair, wash our hair, wash our hair,
> This is the way we wash our hair so early in the morning.   *(mime shampooing hair)*
>
> This is the way we scrub ourselves, scrub ourselves, scrub ourselves,
> This is the way we scrub ourselves so early in the morning.   *(mime washing all over)*
>
> This is the way we dry ourselves, dry ourselves, dry ourselves,
> This is the way we dry ourselves so early in the morning.   *(mime drying with a towel)*

MIX AND MATCH

Additional Picture Books

Appelt, Kathi. *Bubba and Beau Meet the Relatives*. Illustrated by Arthur Howard. Harcourt, 2004.

Bubba the baby and Beau the puppy are thrown into the tub when Mama Pearl and Big Bubba learn that the relatives are coming. Bubba and Beau are mad because they were having so much fun playing in the mud hole. Bubba hates his new tight sailor suit. Bubba and Beau lead cousin Arlene and her dog Bitsy to the mud hole when the adults aren't looking. The adults fill the back of the pickup truck with water and the whole family jumps in.

Esbaum, Jill. *Estelle Takes a Bath*. Illustrated by Mary Newell DePalma. Holt, 2006.

Poor Estelle is enjoying a peaceful bubble bath when a mouse appears on the rim of the tub. Estelle leaps out of the tub in fright. She grabs a broom and chases the mouse. DePalma's tactful illustrations allow Estelle to run around in the buff without offending anyone. The mouse eventually slips in the tub and is in danger of drowning. Estelle rescues the poor mouse, and the two become friends (to the disgust of her cat).

Fox, Christyan, and Diane Fox. *Bathtime PiggyWiggy*. Handprint Books, 2001.

PiggyWiggy likes to pretend in the bathtub. Multiple lift-the-flap pages reveal that PiggyWiggy imagines becoming a deep-sea diver, a water-skier, a long-distance swimmer, a submarine captain, a lifeboat pilot, and a champion surfer. The last lift-the-flap pages reveal that PiggyWiggy would like to sail "around the world with all my friends."

Pelletier, Andrew T. *The Amazing Adventures of Bathman!* Illustrated by Peter Elwell. Dutton, 2005.

"Up in the bathroom, there's a tub of trouble." A little boy tears off his clothes, jumps into the tub, and becomes Bathman. His bath toys tell him that there's been a kidnapping. Cap'n Squeegee has taken Ducky. Bathman dives down past the sharks, Blob the Sponge, and Miss Polly Wog. He rescues Ducky in time for dinner.

Stewart, Amber. *Rabbit Ears*. Illustrated by Laura Rankin. Bloomsbury, 2006.

A little rabbit named Hopscotch hates to have his long ears washed. His mother tries all types of persuasion without success. Hopscotch hides his ears or holds "on to them very, very tightly." One day, Hopscotch's older cousin Bobtail comes for a visit. Hopscotch sees Bobtail washing his own ears and realizes that "big rabbits wash their own ears." He practices washing his stuffed rabbit's ears and then starts in on his own. Have fun singing the little "soapy, soapy, soapy ears" song included.

Additional Songs

"The Bathtub Song." From *Tiny Tunes,* by Carole Peterson. Macaroni Soup, 2005.

"Bubble Bath." From *I Sang It Just for You,* by Mary Kaye. Mary Kaye Music, 2003.

"Bubble Bath Blues." From *Music in My Head,* by Rebecca Frezza. Big Truck, 2002.

"Clean-O." From *Look at My Belly,* by Brady Rymer. Bumblin' Bee, 2002.

"Sailing." From *Pillow Full of Wishes,* by Cathy Fink and Marcy Marxer. Rounder Records, 2000.

"Underwater." From *Underwater,* by Miss Amy. Ionian Productions, 2004.

Creepy Crawlers

PROGRAM AT A GLANCE

Opening Song: "My Favorite Kind of Bugs" from *Giddyup!* by Buck Howdy
Picture Book: *Diary of a Worm* by Doreen Cronin
Story: "Herman the Worm," traditional
Poem/Prop: "Fireflies" from *Fireflies at Midnight* by Marilyn Singer
Picture Book: *Diary of a Spider* by Doreen Cronin
Picture Book: *Aaaarrgghh! Spider!* by Lydia Monks
Poem: "Morning Warming" from *Butterfly Eyes, and Other Secrets of the Meadow*
    by Joyce Sidman
Nursery Rhyme/Movement Activity: "Fiddle Dee Dee," traditional; movement
    idea by Rob Reid
Picture Book: *Diary of a Fly* by Doreen Cronin
Song/Prop: "Shoo Fly," traditional
Picture Book: *Ed Emberley's Bye-Bye, Big Bad Bullybug!* by Ed Emberley
Song/Edible Treat: "Nobody Likes Me," traditional

PREPARATION AND PRESENTATION

Opening Song

"My Favorite Kind of Bugs." From *Giddyup!* by Buck Howdy. Prairie Dog Entertainment, 2005.

Adults will laugh out loud as they hear this song by cowboy crooner Buck Howdy. Buck's favorite kinds of bugs are dead, "whether squished beneath my foot or on the windshield splattered dead."

Picture Book

Diary of a Worm, **by Doreen Cronin. Illustrated by Harry Bliss. HarperCollins, 2003.**

Worm keeps track of his daily life. Adults will particularly enjoy seeing the worms perform "The Hokey Pokey." "You put your head in. You put your head out. You do the hokey pokey and turn yourself about. That's all we could do." The entire audience will giggle when worm tells his older sister that her face looks like her rear end. Along the way, the audience learns how worms help the earth.

Story

"Herman the Worm," traditional.

One can find several different versions of this camp favorite. Most of the versions vary depending on what Herman eats as he grows bigger. The version I have heard the most finds Herman eating his father, mother, sister, and brother. Because this is a family story program, I like to have the family stay intact and opt for the following buggy version.

> I was sitting on a fence post,   *(have everyone slap their knees)*
>
> I was chewing on my bubble gum,   *(have everyone chew-chew-chew)*
>
> Playing with my yo-yo,   *(have everyone mime playing with a yo-yo and whistle)*
>
> When along came Herman the Worm, and he was this big!   *(hold up hands one inch apart)*
>
> And I said, "Herman! What happened?"
>
> And he said, "I ate a fly."
>
> I was sitting on a fence post,   *(have everyone slap their knees)*
>
> I was chewing on my bubble gum,   *(have everyone chew-chew-chew)*
>
> Playing with my yo-yo,   *(have everyone mime playing with a yo-yo and whistle)*
>
> When along came Herman the Worm, and he was this big!   *(hold up hands one foot apart)*
>
> And I said, "Herman! What happened?"
>
> And he said, "I ate a beetle."
>
> I was sitting on a fence post,   *(have everyone slap their knees)*
>
> I was chewing on my bubble gum,   *(have everyone chew-chew-chew)*
>
> Playing with my yo-yo,   *(have everyone mime playing with a yo-yo and whistle)*

When along came Herman the Worm, and he was this big!   *(hold up hands three feet apart)*

And I said, "Herman! What happened?"

And he said, "I ate a caterpillar."

I was sitting on a fence post,   *(have everyone slap their knees)*

I was chewing on my bubble gum,   *(have everyone chew-chew-chew)*

Playing with my yo-yo,   *(have everyone mime playing with a yo-yo and whistle)*

When along came Herman the Worm, and he was this big!   *(hold up hands as far apart as possible)*

And I said, "Herman! What happened?"

And he said, "I ate a tarantula."

I was sitting on a fence post,   *(have everyone slap their knees)*

I was chewing on my bubble gum,   *(have everyone chew-chew-chew)*

Playing with my yo-yo,   *(have everyone mime playing with a yo-yo and whistle)*

When along came Herman the Worm, and he was this big!   *(hold up hands one inch apart again)*

And I said, "Herman! What happened?"

And he said, "I burped."

A different version of "Herman the Worm" can be found on the recording *Mr. Al Concert Live,* by Mr. Al (Cradle Rock, 2004).

Poem/Prop

"Fireflies." From *Fireflies at Midnight,* by Marilyn Singer. Illustrated by Ken Robbins. Atheneum, 2003.

As you read "Fireflies," turn a flashlight on and off with each "flash" mentioned in the poem. There are seven altogether. A firefly is looking for a mate, and the book ends with "flash me back the answer."

Picture Book

***Diary of a Spider,* by Doreen Cronin. Illustrated by Harry Bliss. HarperCollins, 2005.**

Spider's diary entries show Spider's efforts at using playground equipment and failing, taking part in vacuum drills at school ("run like crazy"), making lists of "Things I scare" as well as "Things that scare me," and hanging out with Worm and Fly.

Picture Book

Aaaarrgghh! Spider! **by Lydia Monks. Houghton Mifflin, 2004.**

A spider tries hard to be a human family's pet. Instead, she continuously scares them. Teach your audience to scream "Aaaarrgghh! Spider!" every time the family members in the book react to the spider. The family eventually is impressed with the spider's sparkly webs on the trees in their yard. They make the spider their pet until the spider brings home her friends—and one last chance for your audience to scream.

Poem

"Morning Warming." From *Butterfly Eyes, and Other Secrets of the Meadow,* **by Joyce Sidman. Illustrated by Beth Krommes. Houghton Mifflin, 2006.**

This poem is a riddle that describes a meadow creature and ends with the question "What am I?" Let the audience guess before sharing the answer: a grasshopper. If the audience enjoyed this activity, read "Bubble Song," which describes a spittlebug, and "Ultraviolet," which describes butterflies. Sidman's companion book, *Song of the Water Boatman, and Other Pond Poems* (citation listed in the "Mix and Match" section of this chapter), also contains insect riddle poems.

Nursery Rhyme/Movement Activity

"Fiddle Dee Dee," traditional; movement idea by Rob Reid.

Instruct the adults to stand and sit while making a buzzing noise every time you say the word *fly*. Have the children do the same thing every time you say the word *bumblebee*. Recite the poem slowly the first time. Repeat a second time slightly faster. This is a great activity to get those few adults who are self-conscious when it comes to joining in to participate.

> Fiddle dee dee, fiddle dee dee,
> The *fly* has married the *bumblebee*.
> Said the *fly*, said he,
> "Will you marry me and live with me, sweet *bumblebee?*"
> Fiddle dee dee, fiddle dee dee,
> The *fly* has married the *bumblebee*.

Picture Book

Diary of a Fly, by Doreen Cronin. Illustrated by Harry Bliss. HarperCollins, 2007.

Fly is nervous about starting the first day of school. "What if I'm the only one who eats regurgitated food?" At home, the babysitter (a ladybug) lets eighty-seven of Fly's brothers and sisters get stuck in the flypaper. Fly also examines Worm and Spider through a magnifying glass and realizes he would make an excellent superhero ("I can walk on walls").

Song/Prop

"Shoo Fly," traditional.

I learned this trick from my cousin Richard Efnor. Take a paper bag and hold part of the opening between your thumb and middle finger, as you would when you snap your fingers. If you snap crisply, the bag will sound like something landed inside the bottom. Pass out several lunch-sized paper bags (large grocery bags will also work) and teach the audience members how to snap the bag. The adults and older kids can show the younger children, who might not be able to do the trick. After a few minutes of practice, sing the first verse of the camp song "Shoo Fly" and pretend to follow the path of a fly with your eyes. When you finish the song, snap the bag as if you just caught the fly. Repeat the song and trick one more time so everyone can "catch" his or her fly.

> Shoo fly, don't bother me,
>
> Shoo fly, don't bother me,
>
> Shoo fly, don't bother me,
>
> For I belong to somebody.

The entire version of the song "Shoo Fly" can be found on the recordings *Wee Sing Fun 'n' Folk,* by Pamela Beall and Susan Nipp (Price Stern Sloan, 1989), and *You Are My Flower,* by Elizabeth Mitchell (Last Affair, 1998).

Picture Book

Ed Emberley's Bye-Bye, Big Bad Bullybug! by Ed Emberley. Little, Brown, 2007.

A large alien bug descends from the sky and slowly appears through a series of die-cut holes. He scares the itty-bitty baby bugs with first his eyes, then his teeth, followed by his mouth, ticklers, pinchers, claws, feet, face, and belly. Before the monster bug can eat the baby bugs, he's squashed by a human kid's sneaker. Have fun reading the defiant comments of the baby bugs.

Song/Edible Treat

"Nobody Likes Me," traditional.

Pass out gummy worms. End the program by singing the first verse of this gross-out camp song, which many adults will probably remember from their childhood. After singing it once, invite everyone else to join in before downing their gummy worm.

> Nobody likes me, everybody hates me,
>
> Think I'll go and eat worms.
>
> Long thin skinny ones, short fat juicy ones,
>
> See how they wriggle and squirm.

The entire song can be found on the recordings *Wee Sing Animals, Animals, Animals* (Price Stern Sloan, 1999) and *Wee Sing Silly Songs* (Price Stern Sloan, 1983), both by Pamela Beall and Susan Nipp.

MIX AND MATCH

Additional Picture Books

Bono, Mary. *Ugh! A Bug.* Walker, 2002.

Various children are upset at the presence of flies, spiders, centipedes, worms, ants, beetles, moths, inchworms, ladybugs, fleas, bumblebees, dragonflies, mosquitoes, and more. The narrator warns that bugs are everywhere, so "don't make a fuss—after all, there's a lot more of them than of us."

Harper, Charise Mericle. *Itsy Bitsy the Smart Spider.* Dial, 2004.

When the itsy-bitsy spider is washed out of the spout, she decides "to figure out a way to not get wet again." She makes a deal with a shop owner to catch fleas in exchange for living in a dry place. She also helps the customers. The spider saves up her money to buy an umbrella.

McDonald, Megan. *Beetle McGrady Eats Bugs!* Illustrated by Jane Manning. Greenwillow, 2005.

Beetle McGrady is an adventurous girl. She makes a bet that she can "eat an ant in a second." She practices on raisins but fails to eat the ant. A chef visits her classroom with edible insect treats such as cricket pizza and Mexican stinkbug salsa. Beetle gathers up her courage and eats them. Pass around the picture book afterward and ask the adults in the audience to read aloud "Beetle's Tips for Eating Bugs," found on the endpapers. Here's one example: "When eating a cricket, be sure to check your smile in the mirror. 'Uck! Cricket legs!'"

Palatini, Margie. *The Perfect Pet.* **Illustrated by Bruce Whatley. HarperCollins, 2003.**

"Emily really, really, really wanted a pet." Her parents gave her a plant instead. Emily mentions the virtues of several animals—including a horse, dog, cat, bird, bunny, turtle, fish, guinea pig, and rat. Her parents don't budge on the no-pet rule. Emily finally picks up a bug, names it Doug, and decides it is the perfect pet.

Pinchon, Liz. *The Very Ugly Bug.* **Tiger Tales, 2005.**

A very ugly bug has "huge googly eyes, a lumpy, wibbly-wobbly head, a horrible hairy back, and spotted purple legs." She asks the other bugs why they don't look like her. They explain how their appearances camouflage themselves from predators. When a bird attacks the ugly bug, she wiggles and wobbles and looks even uglier, scaring the bird away. The tagline will especially entertain the adults in the audience when the ugly bug marries another ugly bug and they had "baby bugs who were even uglier than their parents!"

Additional Poems

"Aquatic Fashion," "Diving Beetle's Food-Sharing Rule," "Fly, Dragonfly," and
  "Song of the Water Boatman and the Backswimmer's Refrain." From *Song of the Water Boatman, and Other Pond Poems,* by Joyce Sidman. Illustrated by Beckie Prange. Houghton Mifflin, 2005.

Additional Songs

"The Butterfly Waltz." From *Big Jeff,* by Big Jeff. Big Jeff, 2000.
"Buzzing in the Garden." From *Pizza Pizzaz,* by Peter and Ellen Allard. 80-Z
  Music, 2006.
"Cockroach Conga." From *Spinning Tails,* by Steve Pullara. Cool Beans, 2001.
"Hole in the Ground." From *Under a Big Bright Yellow Umbrella,* by Yosi. Yosi,
  2004.
"Little Spider." From *Fiddlesticks,* by Graham Walker. Laughing Fox Music, 2005.
"Spin Spider Spin." From *The Giggling Dragon,* by Dan Crow. Allshouse, 2005.

Frogs, Snakes, Turtles, 'Gators, and Crocs

PROGRAM AT A GLANCE

Opening Song: "Reptile World" from *Old Enough to Know Better* by Barry Louis
    Polisar
Picture Book: *No Biting, Louise* by Margie Palatini
Chant: "I'm an Alligator," traditional; adapted by Rob Reid
Picture Book: *Class Two at the Zoo* by Julia Jarman
Fingerplay: "Two Old Turtles," traditional
Picture Book: *Hi, Harry!* by Martin Waddell
Picture Book: *Lizard's Home* by George Shannon
Chant: "Froggie," traditional
Picture Book: *Too Many Frogs!* by Sandy Asher
Fingerplay: "Reptiles and Amphibians" by Rob Reid

PREPARATION AND PRESENTATION

Opening Song

**"Reptile World." From *Old Enough to Know Better*, by Barry Louis Polisar.
Rainbow Morning Music, 2005.**

    Play the recording as families enter the program area. Polisar sings about declining an invitation to visit because of all the reptiles scattered throughout the house. Lyrics can be found at Polisar's website: www.barrylou.com/lyricLink .html. Polisar gained more national attention when one of his songs appeared in the 2007 movie *Juno*.

Picture Book

No Biting, Louise, **by Margie Palatini. Illustrated by Matthew Reinhart. HarperCollins, 2007.**

Louise is a young alligator with a biting problem. She bites her father, she bites her sibling, she even bites her grandmother (whose own set of choppers go flying through the air). There's a hilarious succession of animals at the beach that also fall victim to Louise's bites. Heck, Louise even bites the ISBN code on the back cover. She finally outgrows her biting problem only to develop a nasty habit of burping. Adults will enjoy Palatini's writing's casual style: "There was a tendency to . . . how to put it? Gnaw?"

Chant

"I'm an Alligator," traditional; adapted by Rob Reid.

Teach the audience to repeat each stanza back to you with slight pronoun changes.

> **Leader:** I'm an alligator, I'm an alligator,
> Nobody wants to be my friend,   *(point to self)*
> So I guess I'll see you later.

> **Audience:** She's an alligator, she's an alligator,
> Nobody wants to be her friend,   *(audience points to leader)*
> So we guess we'll see you later.

> **Leader:** I'm an alligator, I'm an alligator,
> Nobody wants to play with me,   *(do jumping jacks)*
> So I guess I'll see you later.

> **Audience:** She's an alligator, she's an alligator,
> Nobody wants to play with her,   *(audience does jumping jacks)*
> So we guess we'll see you later.

> **Leader:** I'm an alligator, I'm an alligator,
> Nobody wants to swim with me,   *(make swimming motions)*
> So I guess I'll see you later.

> **Audience:** She's an alligator, she's an alligator,
> Nobody wants to swim with her,   *(audience makes swimming motions)*
> So we guess we'll see you later.

Leader: I'm an alligator, I'm an alligator,

Nobody wants to eat with me,   *(make snapping motion with arms)*

So I guess I'll see you later.

Audience: She's an alligator, she's an alligator,

Nobody wants to eat with her,   *(audience makes snapping motions with arms)*

So we guess we'll see you later.

Picture Book

Class Two at the Zoo, **by Julia Jarman. Illustrated by Lynne Chapman. Carolrhoda, 2007.**

Class Two visits the zoo for a field trip. They are too busy seeing the sights to notice danger. One by one (and sometimes in pairs) the students, and even the teacher, are gobbled by a giant anaconda. A little girl named Molly saves the day by thrusting a stick sideways into the snake's mouth. Class Two marches out again, a little dazed and covered in snake slime.

Fingerplay

"Two Old Turtles," traditional.

Audience members can do this sitting down. Have them do it two times.

Two old turtles going for a walk.   *(hold up two fists, stick out thumbs, move fists slowly forward)*

"Good morning," said one. "Shall we have a little talk?"   *(wiggle one thumb)*

"Yes," said the other. "I do enjoy a chat."   *(wiggle the other thumb)*

So they walked along together with a natter, natter, nat.   *(move fists slowly forward again)*

Picture Book

Hi, Harry! The Moving Story of How One Slow Tortoise Slowly Made a Friend, **by Martin Waddell. Illustrated by Barbara Firth. Candlewick, 2003.**

The subtitle says it all. That friend is Sam Snail. Buster Rabbit, Stan Badger, and Sarah Mouse are too busy to stop for Harry Tortoise. Harry and Sam find each other. Sam and Harry play "Slow Races," "Heads In and Heads Out," and "Turn around and Turn around Again." They talk and talk about "how good it is to be slow." Read the narrative, as well as Harry and Sam's dialogue, with a slow delivery.

Picture Book

Lizard's Home, **by George Shannon. Illustrated by Jose Aruego and Arianne Dewey. Greenwillow, 1999.**

Snake has taken over Lizard's favorite rock. When the bully refuses to budge, Lizard proposes that the two engage in a game of chance to settle their dispute. If Lizard draws the black pebble instead of the white pebble, he wins back his rock. Snake places the pebbles in the bag. Knowing that Snake will no doubt cheat, Lizard comes up with a clever trick and wins back his rock.

Chant

"Froggie," traditional.

Ask the audience to repeat the verses to this fun camp chant.

> Dog!   (Dog!)
> Dog Cat!   (Dog Cat!)
> Dog Cat Mouse!   (Dog Cat Mouse!)
> Froggie!   (Froggie!)
> Itsy-bitsy teensy-weensy little froggie!   (Itsy-bitsy teensy-weensy little froggie!)
> Jump jump jump jump little froggie!   (Jump jump jump jump little froggie!)
> Eating all the itty-bitty worms and spiders!   (Eating all the itty-bitty worms and spiders!)
> Fleas and flies scrumdiddlyicious!   (Fleas and flies scrumdiddlyicious!)
> Ribbit ribbit ribbit ribbit ribbit ribbit ribbit croak!   (Ribbit ribbit ribbit ribbit ribbit ribbit ribbit croak!)

Repeat it three more times—one time in a whisper, one time loud, and the last time in froggielike croaks.

Picture Book

Too Many Frogs! **by Sandy Asher. Illustrated by Keith Graves. Philomel, 2005.**

Rabbit enjoys living a quiet life alone. His solitude is disrupted one night when Froggie invites himself over to hear a story. The next night, Froggie shows up again and makes a snack from Rabbit's kitchen. The third night, Froggie walks in and settles down on Rabbit's pillows. Froggy shows up with his entire family on the fourth night. Rabbit puts his foot down, and Froggie is sorry. Rabbit settles down for the evening but realizes he misses Froggie. Soon, the whole Froggie family is eating snacks and listening to Rabbit (who is clad in a Frog Family Reunion T-shirt) read a story.

Fingerplay

"Reptiles and Amphibians," by Rob Reid.

> Let's pretend we're little frogs
> Sitting on a log in the bog.
> *(Hold up fist sideways, move thumb up and down for mouth, make a frog noise.)*
>
> Let's pretend we're slithery snakes
> Sliding through the canebrake.
> *(Place palms together and move them back and forth.)*
>
> Let's pretend we're a crocodile
> Swimming with a great big smile.
> *(Place palms together and clap.)*
>
> Now we're lizards in the sun
> Now we dart, now we run.
> *(Move pointer finger back and forth.)*
>
> Let's pretend we're turtles eating flies
> Now it's time to say a swamp good-bye.
> *(Make a fist, stick out thumb, wave thumb good-bye.)*

MIX AND MATCH

Additional Picture Books

Bergman, Mara. *Snip Snap! What's That?* Illustrated by Nick Maland. Greenwillow, 2005.

Three children are frightened by an alligator that's crawling into their city apartment. They cry *(have the audience cry)*, and the alligator bites their door *(have the audience make snapping noises)*. The narrator keeps asking, "Were the children scared?" Teach the audience to yell the repetitive refrain, "You bet they were!" When the alligator is very, very close, the children yell at the alligator to get out. Was the alligator scared? Let the audience yell out the answer. "You bet it was!"

Bunting, Eve. *Emma's Turtle*. Illustrated by Marsha Winborn. Boyds Mill, 2007.

Emma's pet turtle decides to go out and see the world. She thinks she's traveling through Africa because she mistakes a tree for an elephant's leg. She imagines she's in Australia when she mistakes a frog for a kangaroo. The neighbor's cat shows up, and the turtle worries it's a tiger in India. Turtle finally returns home and is astonished at the length of his journey.

Fleming, Candace. *Gator Gumbo.* **Illustrated by Sally Anne Lambert. Farrar, Straus & Giroux, 2004.**

Monsieur Gator is very old. He has problems catching food. Mademoiselle Possum, Monsieur Otter, and Madame Skunk all tease him. "She wiggles her striped fanny, puff-puffs her perfume, and asks in a sugarcane voice, 'Do I smell like lunch?'" Monsieur Gator comes up with a plan that will remind older members in the audience of the Little Red Hen story. "Who's gonna fill this pot with water so I can cook up some gumbo?" The other critters reply, "I ain't." The audience can chime in with this frequent refrain. Monsieur Gator eventually tricks the other animals to be the actual recipe ingredients.

McAllister, Angela. *Just like Sisters.* **Illustrated by Sophie Fatus. Atheneum, 2005.**

Nancy, a human child, finally meets her pen pal, Ally (an alligator). The two play together. Ally shows Nancy a photo of her brother, Snap. They go swimming, dancing, and shopping. "I bet people think we're twins." Ally even saves a boy at the beach, although when he sees Ally, he "suddenly remembered how to swim." At the airport, they swap friendship bracelets before Ally returns home.

Rylant, Cynthia. *Alligator Boy.* **Illustrated by Diane Goode. Harcourt, 2007.**

A little boy is tired of being a boy. He goes to the museum and sees a stuffed alligator. His auntie makes him an alligator costume complete with head and tail. Alligator Boy goes to school and does well. He scares the bully and the dogcatcher. "His days were quite happy."

Additional Songs

"All the Little Pollywogs." From *Tuning into Nature,* by Fran Avni. Lemonstone, 2002.

"Echo Gecko." From *A Kid like You,* by Brian Kinder. Brian Kinder, 2002.

"Hippity-Hop." From *Tuning into Nature,* by Fran Avni. Lemonstone, 2002.

"I Got an Alligator." From *Monkey Business,* by Yosi. Yosi, 2002.

"Jumpety Jump." From *Jumpety Jump,* by Graham Walker. Graham Walker, 2001.

"Spyrtle the Turtle." From *Marvelous Day!* by SteveSongs. Rounder Records, 2006.

Jammy Jamboree

PROGRAM AT A GLANCE

Opening Song: "The Moon Is Rising" from *We Wanna Rock* by Thaddeus Rex
Picture Book: *Don't Let the Pigeon Stay Up Late!* by Mo Willems
Picture Book: *Pajama Day* by Lynn Plourde
Movement Activity: "Bedtime Rhyme," traditional; adapted by Rob Reid
Picture Book: *My Daddy Snores* by Nancy H. Rothstein
Sound-Effects Activity: "Funny Snores" by Rob Reid
Picture Book: *Jake Stays Awake* by Michael Wright
Movement Activity: "I'm Not Sleepy" by Rob Reid

PREPARATION AND PRESENTATION

Opening Song

"The Moon Is Rising." From *We Wanna Rock,* by Thaddeus Rex. Thaddeus Rex, 2006.

The kids will join in with the opening line, "Look out / See the moon a-rising," as they enter the story program area. In this song, Thaddeus Rex, a veteran of the PBS show *The Friday Zone,* is not able to fall asleep because he's thinking too much.

Picture Book

***Don't Let the Pigeon Stay Up Late!* by Mo Willems. Hyperion, 2006.**

A pigeon offers several excuses and protestations why it should not go to bed just yet. Many are very creative. "Tell me about your day," "We could count stars," and "Studies show that pigeons hardly need any sleep at all." The pigeon also chants, "Hey, hey! Ho, ho! This here pigeon just won't go!" The adults will recognize many of pigeon's excuses. It's easy to read the pigeon's dialogue with great expression. The pigeon yawns a lot, too, which is sure to trigger yawns in the audience. (I just yawned typing this.)

Picture Book

Pajama Day, by Lynn Plourde. Illustrated by Thor Wickstrom. Dutton, 2005.

Everyone in Mrs. Shepherd's class shows up clad appropriately for Pajama Day except for a student appropriately named Drew A. Blank. "Drew had forgotten what day it was. In fact, Drew might have forgotten his own name if it hadn't been written on his hand as a reminder." Drew also forgot his slippers, breakfast snack, teddy bear, and pillow, but he comes up with creative substitutes. He then participates in several after-school activities. He's so exhausted that he forgets to put on his pajamas at the end of the day.

Movement Activity

"Bedtime Rhyme," traditional; adapted by Rob Reid.

> *(Instruct the girls and moms to act out the motions to the first section.)*
> This little girl is going to bed.   *(point to self)*
> Down on the bed she lays her head.   *(place head on hands)*
> She wraps herself in her blanket tight.   *(wrap arms around self)*
> And this is the way she sleeps tonight.   *(remain in this position through
>   the next section)*
>
> *(Instruct the boys and dads to act out the motions for this next section.)*
> This little boy is going to bed.   *(point to self)*
> Down on the bed he lays his head.   *(place head on hands)*
> He wraps himself in his blanket tight.   *(wrap arms around self)*
> And this is the way he sleeps tonight.
>
> *(Everyone acts out the motions for the last section.)*
> Morning comes, they open their eyes.   *(head up, rub eyes)*
> Off with a toss, the blanket flies.   *(fling arms in the air)*
> Soon they are up, dressed and away.   *(jump up)*
> Ready to run around all day.   *(let everyone run in circles for a few minutes)*

Picture Book

My Daddy Snores, **by Nancy H. Rothstein. Illustrated by Stephen Gilpin. Scholastic, 2007.**

Daddy's snores boom like a dinosaur's roars, rumble like an earthquake, chug like a train, buzz like a bumblebee, whistle like a teapot, and honk like a truck. "Mommy played 'Musical Beds.'" She moves into the baby's crib, but it breaks. She sleeps in the bathtub, but the faucet drips water on her head. She even tries sleeping in the hamster's cage and the doghouse without success. She makes Daddy sleep outside in a tent, but his snores wake up the birds. Daddy visits a doctor, who helps cure the snoring. Everything is peaceful until Daddy starts talking in his sleep.

Sound-Effects Activity

"Funny Snores," by Rob Reid.

Encourage the audience to use their imagination coming up with different sounds for a variety of snores. Start with the snores in *My Daddy Snores.* Make a snore that sounds like a dinosaur. Move on to earthquake, train, bumblebee, teapot whistle, and truck. Think of other snoring-sound possibilities. How would a cat snore? ("Snore, meow, meow, snore, meow, meow.") How about a cow, pig, or snake? ("Hiss snort, hiss snort.")

Picture Book

Jake Stays Awake, **by Michael Wright. Feiwel and Friends, 2007.**

The parents in the audience will quickly recognize this scenario. Young Jake is adamant: "'Unless I can sleep with my parents,' he said, 'I won't close my eyes, and I won't go to bed!'" His parents give in, and he climbs in the bed made for two. There's little room for all three. They decide to stretch out on the roof. That doesn't work, so they sleep on the stairs, then the bathtub, the kitchen counter, the garbage cans, and the car. Jake comes up with a great idea. His own bed!

Movement Activity

"I'm Not Sleepy," by Rob Reid.

Have the audience members sit and pretend they are lying in bed. Start reciting this call-and-response chant and add motions until everyone is doing several motions at once.

> I'm not sleepy,   (I'm not sleepy,)
> Blinking my eyes.   (Blinking my eyes.)
> *(Blink eyes.)*

I'm not sleepy,   (I'm not sleepy,)
Wiggling my feet,   (Wiggling my feet,)
Blinking my eyes.   (Blinking my eyes.)
(Wiggle feet, blink eyes.)

I'm not sleepy,   (I'm not sleepy,)
Waving both hands,   (Waving both hands,)
Wiggling my feet,   (Wiggling my feet,)
Blinking my eyes.   (Blinking my eyes.)
(Wave hands, wiggle feet, blink eyes.)

I'm not sleepy,   (I'm not sleepy,)
Twisting my waist,   (Twisting my waist,)
Waving both hands,   (Waving both hands,)
Wiggling my feet,   (Wiggling my feet,)
Blinking my eyes.   (Blinking my eyes.)
(Add twisting motion to the other motions.)

I'm not sleepy,   (I'm not sleepy,)
Tossing my head,   (Tossing my head,)
Twisting my waist,   (Twisting my waist,)
Waving both hands,   (Waving both hands,)
Wiggling my feet,   (Wiggling my feet,)
Blinking my eyes.   (Blinking my eyes.)
(Add tossing motion to the other motions.)

I'm VERY sleepy!   (I'm VERY sleepy!)
Gonna yawn,   (Gonna yawn,)
(Stop doing all other motions. Yawn and stretch arms.)
And gonna snore.   (And gonna snore.)
(Everyone closes eyes, slumps in chair, and snores.)

MIX AND MATCH

Additional Picture Books

Di Pucchio, Kelly. *Bed Hogs.* Illustrated by Howard Fine. Hyperion, 2004.

A family of hogs sleep piled on top of each other. Little Runt is stuck on the bottom. Sister Rose sticks her stinky feet in Little Runt's face, so he kicks her off the pile. He does the same to the other sleeping pigs, one by one, until he's the only one left on the straw bed. He's cold and lonely and hollers, "Without y'all hoggin' up the bed, I'll *never* get to sleep!" They quickly rejoin him.

Perl, Erica S. *Chicken Bedtime Is Really Early.* Illustrated by George Bates. Abrams, 2005.

At five o'clock, baby chicks get ready for bed. We even see one chick flossing its beak. They are asleep by six o'clock. At seven o'clock, the cows and sheep start to go to bed. At eight o'clock, it's the bunny rabbits' turn. They even wear footy pajamas. The fish get ready at nine o'clock. Fish with teeth brush, and those without gargle. One fish dad states, "No more carping" when the little fish try to stall bedtime. The performing frogs take a five-minute break at ten o'clock and then get ready for bed. The hamsters sleep at eleven o'clock but are back at the wheel at midnight—totally refreshed. The rooster gets up at four in the morning and does his exercises (complete with barbells) before waking everyone else up.

Peters, Lisa Westberg. *Sleepyhead Bear.* Illustrated by Ian Schoenherr. Greenwillow, 2006.

It's hot outside, and Bear wants "to catch a few winks in his lair." He is bothered by buzzing bugs. Bear runs outside and jumps in the pond, but he's bothered by frogs and other insects. He climbs a tree, where he runs into bees. He tumbles into a meadow full of flowers. He discovers that butterflies "don't buzz or sting or whir." Instead, they tickle him. He's happy and plays with them for hours until he falls asleep with fireflies twinkling around him.

Waber, Bernard. *The Mouse That Snored.* Houghton Mifflin, 2000.

A quiet man, his quiet wife, and their quiet pets live in a country home. The members of this household rarely speak, and they chew "quiet food," like mashed potatoes and bread pudding. A noisy mouse enters the house, raids the pantry, falls asleep, snores, and wakes up everyone else. The snores shake the building. When the mouse wakes up, he charms the quiet family, who let him stay, despite the snoring.

Warnes, Tim. *Can't You Sleep, Dotty?* Tiger Tales, 2001.

Dotty the dog has trouble sleeping the first night in a new home. She shifts positions but winds up howling and waking the other household pets. They suggest she try counting stars (she can only count to one), have a drink (she makes "a tiny puddle"), and hide under her blanket. None of the ideas work, causing her (and hopefully your audience) to howl even more. She eventually snuggles in with her new friends and falls asleep.

Wilson, Karma. *Sleepyhead.* **Illustrated by John Segal. McElderry, 2006.**
   A cat tries to get a tiny teddy bear to go to bed. The teddy comes up with many excuses. Ask the children (with help from the adults) to mime the following: one more book, one more hug, one more kiss, one more drink, one more cuddle, one more story, one more stretch, and one more yawn. Ask the adults in the audience to shake their fingers with every "It's time for bed."

Additional Songs

"Dream Dream Dream." From *Hey, Picasso,* by Jessica Harper. Rounder Records, 2004.
"Goin' to Bed Early Blues." From *Stinky Feet,* by Steve Cosgrove. Hiccup, 2002.
"Goodnight Moon." From *Happy Songs,* by Milkshake. Milkshake, 2002.
"Not Naptime." From *Not Naptime,* by Justin Roberts. Justin Roberts, 2002.
"T.I.R.E.D." From *Celebrate: A Song Resource,* by Stuart Stotts and Tom Pease. Tomorrow River Music, 2000.
"Why Kids Sing to Their Parents." From *The Town around the Bend,* by Bill Harley. Round River Records, 2003.

Meow and Squeak!

PROGRAM AT A GLANCE

Opening Song: "Mouse in the House" from *Reggae Playground* by Marty Dread
Sound-Effects Activity: "Mice and Cat Practice"
Fingerplay: "The Kitty and the Mouse," traditional; adapted by Rob Reid
Picture Book: *Crackers* by Becky Bloom
Song/Felt Board: "Where, Oh Where Has My Little Mouse Gone?" traditional;
    adapted by Rob Reid
Picture Book: *Scaredy Mouse* by Alan MacDonald
Poem: "Cat and Mouse" by Eric Ode from *Rolling in the Aisles: A Collection of
    Laugh-Out-Loud Poems*
Song: "What Kind of Cat Are You?" from *What Kind of Cat Are You?* by Billy
    Jonas
Picture Book: *All for Pie, Pie for All* by David Martin
Song: "T-A-B-B-Y," traditional; adapted by Rob Reid
Picture Book/Movement Activity: *Mabela the Clever* by Margaret Read
    MacDonald
Poem: "Cat Talk" from *Cat Poems* by Dave Crawley

PREPARATION AND PRESENTATION

Opening Song

"Mouse in the House." From *Reggae Playground,* by Marty Dread. Putumayo,
2006.

Start things off with this reggae-influenced ditty describing a mouse appearing throughout different locations in the house. Marty Dread provides the vocals from this anthology released by the popular Putumayo label.

Sound-Effects Activity

"Mice and Cat Practice"

Once the audience is seated, discuss the long rivalry between cats and mice. Tell them that you're going to need help making cat meows and mouse squeaks at various points throughout the storytime. Ask them to demonstrate their sound-effects abilities now.

Fingerplay

"The Kitty and the Mouse," traditional; adapted by Rob Reid.

I borrowed this fingerplay from the first *Family Storytime* book. My audiences had loud, squealing fun with the traditional fingerplay "The Puppy and the Cat," in which one's "dog fist" chases one's "cat fist." I changed a few characters to fit this theme and made it a two-person activity. Have an adult pair up with a child. Repeat if necessary so that all children have a turn. Adults and kids can change roles, too.

> See the little mouse,　*(child holds up fist to represent the "mouse")*
>
> See the kitty cat,　*(adult holds up fist to represent the "cat")*
>
> Kitty goes to sleep—just like that.　*(adult closes eyes and lowers head as if asleep)*
>
> Mousie sneaks up quietly,　*(child slowly brings "mouse" fist next to adult's "cat" fist)*
>
> Tickles Kitty's chin!　*(child tickles "cat" fist)*
>
> Kitty wakes up startled!　*(adult "wakes up")*
>
> Let the chase begin!　*("cat" fist chases "mouse" fist)*

Picture Book

Crackers, by Becky Bloom. Illustrated by Pascal Biet. Orchard Books, 2001.

Crackers the cat looks for a job. He works as a warehouse security guard but is fired for giving scrap wood to a mouse. He next gets a job working at a resort marina but is once again fired for helping a family of mice. His job as a waiter doesn't fare any better as he's fired for seating a couple of mice. He eventually gets a job working in a mouse-owned cheese shop, thanks to his wonderful references—all of the mice he helped in his previous jobs.

Song/Felt Board

"Where, Oh Where Has My Little Mouse Gone?" traditional; adapted by Rob Reid.

Mention that the mice in the last story were lucky to find a cat that liked mice. Some cats like mice for other reasons. Make a felt mouse and a felt cat beforehand. Place the mouse on the felt board as you begin to sing this adaptation of "Where, Oh Where Has My Little Dog Gone?"

> Where, oh where has my little mouse gone?
> Oh where, oh where can he be?
> With his cute little ears and his tail so long,
> Oh where, oh where can he be?

Make a meow noise, place the cat felt character over the mouse character and burp. Look at the audience with a surprised look and ask, "You don't suppose . . . ?" Hold up the next picture book and state, "Oh, here's the mouse—starring in his own picture book."

Picture Book

Scaredy Mouse, **by Alan MacDonald. Illustrated by Tim Warnes. Tiger Tales, 2002.**

A young mouse named Squeak is "a scared mouse, a stay-at-home mouse." He worries about the cat. His sister Nibbles securely ties Squeak to string so he doesn't get lost. She then leads him out of the mouse hole to find cake. Squeak thinks he sees the cat and yells, "It's the cat! It's the cat!" It turns out to be a scarf. This happens over and over. Squeak mistakes something for the cat and runs screaming. Ask the audience to yell, "It's the cat! It's the cat!" along with Squeak. Of course, the real cat eventually shows up and is ready to grab both mice. Squeak's string tangles the cat, and Squeak is no longer afraid.

Poem

"Cat and Mouse," by Eric Ode. From *Rolling in the Aisles: A Collection of Laugh-Out-Loud Poems,* **edited by Bruce Lansky. Meadowbrook, 2004.**

Mice find cats ill-bred, while cats like mice. They think they taste like chicken.

Song

"What Kind of Cat Are You?" From *What Kind of Cat Are You?* **by Billy Jonas. Bang-a-Bucket, 2002.**

This is one of the few songs I would play and let the audience sit quietly and listen to the whole song. The youngest children might squirm, but the older kids and the adults will appreciate the wordplay. Everyone will probably join in on the catchy chorus. Jonas asks a series of cat riddles to which kids on the recording answer. Here are two examples: "What kind of cat is a chocolate candy bar? Kit Kat!" and "What kind of cat is a whole bunch of cows? Cattle." The kids on the recording are quite endearing, especially the child who answers the riddle "What kind of cat is connected to the engine of your car? Catalytic converter." There are twenty-seven riddles. You may want to write the answers on strips of poster board and hold them up as they're mentioned in the song.

Picture Book

All for Pie, Pie for All, **by David Martin. Illustrated by Valeri Gorbachev. Candlewick, 2006.**

Grandmother Cat bakes an apple pie, and the cat family enjoys it, slice by slice. While the cats are napping, the mouse family eats the leftovers, piece by piece. While the mice nap, the ants eat the crumbs, crumb by crumb. Grandmother Cat asks if she should bake another apple pie. Here's where the audience can let loose with their cat and mouse noises. When the cats in the story say yes to Grandmother Cat's question, the audience can meow in response. The mice squeak yes also. Ask the audience to squeak. The ants also say yes to Grandmother Cat. The audience can say yes in high-pitched "ant" voices.

Song

"T-A-B-B-Y," traditional; adapted by Rob Reid.

Change the traditional song "B-I-N-G-O" to feature a cat. As you take away each letter, substitute "Meow."

> There was a farmer had a cat and Tabby was its name-o.
> T-A-B-B-Y, T-A-B-B-Y, T-A-B-B-Y, and Tabby was its name-o.
>
> There was a farmer had a cat and Tabby was its name-o.
> (Meow)-A-B-B-Y, (Meow)-A-B-B-Y, (Meow)-A-B-B-Y, and Tabby was its name-o.
>
> There was a farmer had a cat and Tabby was its name-o.
> (Meow-meow)-B-B-Y, (Meow-meow)-B-B-Y, (Meow-meow)-B-B-Y, and Tabby was its name-o.
>
> There was a farmer had a cat and Tabby was its name-o.
> (Meow-meow-meow)-B-Y, (Meow-meow-meow)-B-Y, (Meow-meow-meow)-B-Y, and Tabby was its name-o.

There was a farmer had a cat and Tabby was its name-o.

(Meow-meow-meow-meow)-Y, (Meow-meow-meow-meow)-Y,
(Meow-meow-meow-meow)-Y, and Tabby was its name-o.

There was a farmer had a cat and Tabby was its name-o.

(Meow-meow-meow-meow-meow), (Meow-meow-meow-meow-
meow), (Meow-meow-meow-meow-meow), and Tabby was its
name-o.

When everyone is done with the song, I usually launch into this verse:

There was a farmer had a mouse and Mickey was his name-o.

M-I-C-K-E-Y . . . *(sing this last line in Mickey Mouse's trademark falsetto)*

It gets a laugh, and I encourage the families to try the whole thing on the ride or walk home.

The traditional song "B-I-N-G-O" can be found on several recordings, including the following:

Beall, Pamela, and Susan Nipp. *Wee Sing Animals, Animals, Animals.* Price Stern Sloan, 1999.

Coffey, James. *Animal Groove.* Blue Vision, 1999.

Sharon, Lois, and Bram. *Great Big Hits 2.* Elephant Records, 2002.

Picture Book/Movement Activity

Mabela the Clever, by Margaret Read MacDonald. Illustrated by Tim Coffey. Whitman, 2001.

Mabela was a clever mouse. Her father gave her lots of good advice. Mabela uses that advice when the cat tricks the other mice into joining the "Cat Club." I was lucky to be part of a group that got to be in the line of mice under Margaret Read MacDonald's live direction and telling. She gives advice on how to have the audience participate with the story in the book's front matter. The audience members can be the mice singing a song (words and melody provided) while marching in a line. One person is the cat, who catches the last mouse in line every time the mice sing "Fo Feng."

Poem

"Cat Talk." From *Cat Poems,* by David Crawley. Boyds Mill, 2005.

End the program with this short poem that compares cats that simply say "Meow" with the alley cat, who lets out a loud "Mee-YOWL!" Have everyone meow and squeak one last time.

MIX AND MATCH

Additional Picture Books

Crimi, Carolyn. *Tessa's Tip-Tapping Toes.* **Illustrated by Marsha Gray Carrington. Orchard, 2002.**

Tessa the mouse loves to dance. Her mother forbids her to dance lest she catch the attention of the new cat. Oscar (the new cat) loves to sing. His owner forbids him to sing so as not to disturb the neighbors. Tessa and Oscar learn about each other's talents, and soon the whole household is dancing and singing.

Egielski, Richard. *Slim and Jim.* **HarperCollins, 2002.**

Buster the one-eyed cat employs Slim, a down-and-out rat, to steal some jewels. Slim refuses at the last minute. A mouse named Jim tries to help Slim. The two become great friends. One day, Buster kidnaps Slim. The two friends use their skills to defeat the evil cat.

Hoberman, Mary Ann. *Two Sillies.* **Harcourt, 2000.**

Silly Lilly wants a cat just like Sammy's. Sammy tells her how to get her own cat. He leads her through an elaborate process of cutting trees, building a shed, buying a cow, and, finally, milking it. A stray cat shows up for the milk, and that's how Silly Lilly got her cat. Mice invade the shed. Lilly shows Sammy how to get rid of them. He makes a bed of hay in the shed. He removes the cow. Without the milk, the cat eats the mice and slumbers on the hay. That's one way to get rid of mice.

Lakin, Patricia. *Clarence the Copy Cat.* **Illustrated by John Manders. Doubleday, 2002.**

Clarence sticks to his principles—he will not hurt mice. His owners kick him out. Clarence finds a new home at the local library. When a mouse shows up, the librarian tells Clarence to get it. Clarence tries his best to get rid of the mouse without harming it. The cat accidentally gets caught in the copy machine, which makes a copy of him looking fierce and wild. The mouse never returns after seeing that copy of Clarence.

Additional Songs

"Barn Cat." From *Fiddlesticks,* by Graham Walker. Laughing Fox Music, 2005.

"A Cat's like That." From *The Giggling Dragon,* by Dan Crow. Allshouse, 2005.

"Country Mouse and City Mouse." From *Magic Parade,* by Elizabeth McMahon. Mrs. McPuppet, 2006.

"The Library Cat." From *King Kong Chair,* by Rick Charette. Pine Point Records, 2004.

"Malcolm McGillikitty." From *At the Bottom of the Sea,* by Ralph's World. Mini Fresh, 2002.

"Mouse Jamboree." From *Mouse Jamboree,* by Mary Kaye. Mary Kaye Music, 2004.

Mouthsounds

PROGRAM AT A GLANCE

Opening Song: "What Do You Hear?" from *My Mama Was a Train* by James Coffey

Picture Book: *Pssst!* by Adam Rex

Song: "I Know a Song That Gets on Your Nerves," traditional; adapted by Rob Reid

Picture Book: *Noises at Night* by Beth Raisner Glass and Susan Lubner

Picture Book: *Roar of a Snore* by Marsha Diane Arnold

Poem: "The Duck" from *Hippopotamus Stew, and Other Silly Animal Poems* by Joan Horton

Song: "Moosie, Moosie," traditional; adapted by Rob Reid

Picture Book: *Clip-Clop* by Nicola Smee

Song: "Once an Austrian Went Yodeling," traditional

Picture Book: *Waking Up Wendell* by April Stevens

PREPARATION AND PRESENTATION

Opening Song

"What Do You Hear?" From *My Mama Was a Train,* by James Coffey. Blue Vision Music, 2002.

As folks enter the story program area, they'll automatically start grooving to Coffey's tune. They'll also make the sound effects while waiting for the program to begin: whistles blowing, bells ringing, and more. Coffey excels at songs about transportation.

Picture Book

Pssst! **by Adam Rex. Harcourt, 2007.**

This is the funniest picture book published in 2007. As a child walks through the zoo, the various animals attract her attention with a "Pssst" noise. They all have strange requests. The gorilla wants a new tire, the javelina wants trash cans, the bats want flashlights, the penguins want paint (their exhibit isn't bright enough), the sloths want bicycle helmets (they fall on the ground), the turkeys want corn (not to eat but "to turn it into a clean-burning fuel"), and the baboon and tortoise suggest she get a wheelbarrow to haul everything (they give her coins that the peacock retrieved from the fountains). Be sure to read the many signs in the zoo, including "I Am the Walrus (koo-koo-kachoo)" and "Camel-Lot (1 Hump or 2)."

Song

"I Know a Song That Gets on Your Nerves," traditional; adapted by Rob Reid.

Sing this noisy, irritating song to "Mary Had a Little Lamb" and sing it until various audience members cover their ears. (It won't take long—I speak from experience.)

> I know a song that gets on your nerves,
>
> Gets on your nerves, gets on your nerves,
>
> I know a song that gets on your nerves,
>
> And this is how it goes . . .   *(repeat)*

Picture Book

Noises at Night, **by Beth Raisner Glass and Susan Lubner. Illustrated by Bruce Whatley. Abrams, 2005.**

A young boy hears noises at night and lets his imagination go wild in a fun way. The "Whieeee, Whieeee" of the wind inspires the boy to pretend he's a policeman blowing a whistle to direct traffic. The "Ticcckk, Toccckk" of the clock has him imagining he's a cowboy, and the noise makes the sound of his horse trotting. Let the audience perform all of the noises the boy hears: the wind, the clock, the dripping faucet, the hiss of the heater, thunder, a falling branch, traffic, and the creak of his bed. The final sound is silence, and let the story end with everyone in the audience being as quiet as can be. In the back matter, illustrator Whatley discusses the moments of humor he adds "that appeal to kids one minute and the parents the next."

Picture Book

Roar of a Snore, **by Marsha Diane Arnold. Illustrated by Pierre Pratt. Dial, 2006.**

Jack is awoken by "a thundering, ear-splitting, roar of a snore!" He checks out the various family members to see who is responsible. Everyone—including old hound dog Blue, Mama Gwyn, Sweet Baby Sue, Papa Ben, the twins, and the farm animals—makes his or her own special snore. They aren't the source of the largest of snores, however. That distinction belongs to a stray kitten. The family settles down to sleep near the kitten in the haystack. Unfortunately, they wake up Molly Olson down the road. There are several opportunities for the audience to make a wide array of snoring sounds. Have the moms in the audience snore for Mama Gwyn, the dads snore for Papa Ben, the kids for Sweet Baby Sue and the twins, and everyone for the animals.

Poem

"The Duck." From *Hippopotamus Stew, and Other Silly Animal Poems,* by Joan Horton. Illustrated by JoAnn Adinolfi. Holt, 2006.

Several birds make different bird noises. The duck, however, has problems. Hold up a toy rubber duck as you read the line "Perhaps I'd have a lot more luck / If I were not a rubber duck."

Song

"Moosie, Moosie," traditional; adapted by Rob Reid.

Sing this short call-and-response camp song three times, louder and louder each time. Sing the song a fourth time, whispering the first three lines and then yelling the "La la la la la la la!"

> Moosie, moosie!   (Moosie, moosie!)
> A riki tiki moosie!   (A riki tiki moosie!)
> A moosa moosa moosie!   (A moosa moosa moosie!)
> La la la la la la la!   (La la la la la la la!)

Picture Book

Clip-Clop, **by Nicola Smee. Boxer Books, 2006.**

A horse takes a cat, dog, pig, and duck for a ride. Have everyone in the audience slap their legs whenever you read "Clip-clop, clippity-clop." The animals urge the horse to go faster and faster. The audience should also speed up their slapping until the animals fall off the horse into a haystack. Have the audience make popping noises with their fingers inside their cheeks as the animals land with "Plop! Plop! Ploppity-plop!" Of course, the animals want to ride again, so end the story with more leg slapping. Feel free to improvise at the end by pretending the horse goes faster and slower.

Song

"Once an Austrian Went Yodeling," traditional.

This active, noisy song can be found on the following recordings:

Beall, Pamela, and Susan Nipp. *Wee Sing Silly Songs*. Price Stern Sloan, 1982.

Byers, Kathy. *'Round the Campfire*. KT Music, 2004. (Listed as "Austrian Folk Song.")

Teach folks to slap their legs on the words, "Ho-li-ah" and to slap legs, clap, and snap fingers on the words, "Ho-le-rah-hi-hi-ah." Many adults will know the song from their childhood.

Once an Austrian went yodeling on a mountain so high,

When he met with an avalanche interrupting his cry.

Ho-li-ah, Ho-le-rah-hi-hi-ah!

Ho-le-rah cuckoo-cuckoo. Rumble, rumble!   *(roll hands over and over on "Rumble, rumble")*

Ho-le-rah-hi-hi-ah!

Ho-le-rah cuckoo-cuckoo. Rumble, rumble!

Ho-le-rah-hi-hi-ah!

Ho-le-rah cuckoo-cuckoo. Rumble, rumble!

Ho-le-rah-hi-hi-ah!

Ho-le-rah cuckoo-cuckoo. Rumble, rumble!

Once an Austrian went yodeling on a mountain so high,

When he met with a skier interrupting his cry.

Ho-li-ah, Ho-le-rah-hi-hi-ah!

Ho-le-rah cuckoo-cuckoo. Swoosh, swoosh! Rumble, rumble!   *(add skiing pole motions on "Swoosh, swoosh")*

Ho-le-rah-hi-hi-ah!

Ho-le-rah cuckoo-cuckoo. Swoosh, swoosh! Rumble, rumble!

Ho-le-rah-hi-hi-ah!

Ho-le-rah cuckoo-cuckoo. Swoosh, swoosh! Rumble, rumble!

Ho-le-rah-hi-hi-ah!

Ho-le-rah cuckoo-cuckoo. Swoosh, swoosh! Rumble, rumble!

Once an Austrian went yodeling on a mountain so high,

When he met with a St. Bernard interrupting his cry.

Ho-li-ah, Ho-le-rah-hi-hi-ah!

Ho-le-rah cuckoo-cuckoo. Woof, woof! Swoosh, swoosh! Rumble, rumble!   *(add hands up for paws)*

Ho-le-rah-hi-hi-ah!

Ho-le-rah cuckoo-cuckoo. Woof, woof! Swoosh, swoosh! Rumble, rumble!

Ho-le-rah-hi-hi-ah!

Ho-le-rah cuckoo-cuckoo. Woof, woof! Swoosh, swoosh! Rumble, rumble!

Ho-le-rah-hi-hi-ah!

Ho-le-rah cuckoo-cuckoo. Woof, woof! Swoosh, swoosh! Rumble, rumble!

Once an Austrian went yodeling on a mountain so high,

When he met with a grizzly bear interrupting his cry.

Ho-li-ah, Ho-le-rah-hi-hi-ah!

Ho-le-rah cuckoo-cuckoo. Grrr, grrr! Woof, woof! Swoosh, swoosh! Rumble, rumble!   *(add hands up for claws)*

Ho-le-rah-hi-hi-ah!

Ho-le-rah cuckoo-cuckoo. Grrr, grrr! Woof, woof! Swoosh, swoosh! Rumble, rumble!

Ho-le-rah-hi-hi-ah!

Ho-le-rah cuckoo-cuckoo. Grrr, grrr! Woof, woof! Swoosh, swoosh! Rumble, rumble!

Ho-le-rah-hi-hi-ah!

Ho-le-rah cuckoo-cuckoo. Grrr, grrr! Woof, woof! Swoosh, swoosh! Rumble, rumble!

Once an Austrian went yodeling on a mountain so high,

When he met with a pretty girl interrupting his cry.

Ho-li-ah, Ho-le-rah-hi-hi-ah!

Ho-le-rah cuckoo-cuckoo. Kiss, kiss! Grrr, grrr! Woof, woof! Swoosh, swoosh! Rumble, rumble!   *(add puckering lips and make kissing noises)*

Ho-le-rah-hi-hi-ah!

Ho-le-rah cuckoo-cuckoo. Kiss, kiss! Grrr, grrr! Woof, woof! Swoosh,
swoosh! Rumble, rumble!

Ho-le-rah-hi-hi-ah!

Ho-le-rah cuckoo-cuckoo. Kiss, kiss! Grrr, grrr! Woof, woof! Swoosh,
swoosh! Rumble, rumble!

Ho-le-rah-hi-hi-ah!

Ho-le-rah cuckoo-cuckoo. Kiss, kiss! Grrr, grrr! Woof, woof! Swoosh,
swoosh! Rumble, rumble!

A fun version featuring different musical instruments can be found on Miss
Amy's recording *Wide Wide World* (Ionian Productions, 2005) under the title
"Once an Austrian."

Picture Book

Waking Up Wendell, **by April Stevens. Illustrated by Tad Hills. Schwartz &
Wade, 2007.**

End the program with this picture book that features a wonderful array
of noises for the audience to make. A bird chirps ("Tweet-Tweet-Ta-Ta-Ta-
Tweeeeet") and wakes up Mr. Krudwig, who then lets his dog outside. The dog
barks ("Rappity-rappity-rap! Rappity-rappity-rap!") and wakes up his neighbor
Mrs. Musky. Each household makes a noise that wakes up the next-door neighbors.
The audience can participate in a call-and-response way for each sound effect
and bit of dialogue. The various noises include a sewing machine, harmonica,
teakettle, phone, singing in the shower, and more. My favorite is the cat who bats
the screen door back and forth with a "Wack-Slam! Wack-Slam!" The last one to
wake up is baby Wendell, who says, "Weeeeeee!"

MIX AND MATCH

Additional Picture Books

Dodd, Emma. *Dog's Noisy Day.* Dutton, 2003.

Dog wakes up with a "Yawn" and "Woof! Woof!" and heads outside. He
encounters several animals, including a rooster, cows, a donkey, pigs, ducks, bees,
and sheep. Of course, all of the animals make a lot of noise. Dog knows it's time
to go home when he hears the "Twit-A-Woo" of an owl.

Gerstein, Mordicai. *Carolinda Clatter!* Roaring Brook, 2005.

Over the years, a giant falls asleep and turns into a mountain. Eventually, a
village is built near the mountain and everyone is quiet, fearful of waking the

giant. "There was no music. No one even sneezed. The animals were quiet too—no moos or barks." Once little Carolinda is born, everything changes. She is very, very noisy and wakes up the giant.

Harper, Jessica. *Nora's Room*. Illustrated by Lindsay Harper duPont. HarperCollins, 2001.

Nora is upstairs in her bedroom making a racket. Her mom, siblings, and pets are on the first floor trying to describe the noise coming from Nora's room. It sounds like the city zoo animals are free. It sounds "like London Bridge is REALLY falling down!" It sounds like a rodeo. When Nora's mother asks, "What's going on in there?" Nora replies, "Oh, nothing." The book is based on Harper's song from her recording *Nora's Room* (Alacazam, 1996).

MacDonald, Margaret Read. *The Squeaky Door*. Illustrated by Mary Newell DePalma. HarperCollins, 2006.

MacDonald's lively version of this traditional cumulative tale has several kissing noises, crying noises, repetitive lines (such as "No. Not me"), animal sound effects, and, of course, several opportunities for the audience to make the biggest, loudest "Squeeeak" when Grandma shuts the door. Have special fun making the noise of the oilcan, "Glub . . . glub . . . glub . . . glub," interspersed with the squeaking noise and the final "Ahhhmmmmmm" as everyone falls asleep.

Wheeler, Lisa. *Old Cricket*. Illustrations by Ponder Goembel. Atheneum, 2003.

Lazy Old Cricket tries to get out of work by complaining about the creak in his knee. Ask the audience to repeat "creak-creak-creak" when Old Cricket walks. He adds a "crick-crick-crick" to his neck to get out of helping Cousin Katydid and a "crack-crack-crack" in his back to avoid helping the ants. Old Crow appears with a "caw-caw-caw" and tries to make a meal out of Old Cricket, who then develops some hiccups—"hic-hic-hic." The adults will also enjoy the frequent variations of the line "You don't get to be an old cricket by being a dumb bug."

Additional Songs

"A-E-I-O and U." From *Scat like That*, by Cathy Fink and Marcy Marxer. Rounder Records, 2005.

"Clap, Snap and Whistle." From *Do You Wish You Could Fly?* by Kathy Byers. KT Music, 2000.

"Do the Pet Sounds." From *Pet Sounds*, by Gary Rosen. GMR, 2005.

"Everybody Clap Your Hands." From *Stinky Cake*, by Carole Peterson. Macaroni Soup, 2005.

"I Love Playing the Kazoo." From *Making Good Noise*, by Tom Chapin. Sundance, 2003.

"I've Got a Friend (He Won't Be Quiet)." From *My Best Day*, by Trout Fishing in America. Trout, 2006.

The Name Game

PROGRAM AT A GLANCE

Opening Song: "Your Name Backwards" from *InFINity* by Trout Fishing in America
Riddles: *What's in a Name? A Book of Name Jokes* by Jill L. Donahue
Picture Book: *Four Boys Named Jordan* by Jessica Harper
Picture Book: *Catalina Magdalena Hoopensteiner Wallendiner Hogan Logan Bogan Was Her Name* by Tedd Arnold
Song: "Lisa Lee Elizabeth" from *Imagine That* by Monty Harper
Picture Book: *My Name Is Yoon* by Helen Recorvits
Picture Book: *Matthew A.B.C.* by Peter Catalanotto
Chant: "Yon Yonson," traditional
Picture Book: *No, David!* by David Shannon
Art Activity: *No, David!* Scenes

PREPARATION AND PRESENTATION

Opening Song

"Your Name Backwards." From *InFINity*, by Trout Fishing in America. Trout, 2001.

Keith Grimwood and Ezra Idle, the duo who make up Trout Fishing in America, are two of the funniest children's entertainers on the market. Folks entering the story program area will be delighted as they hear these two put a spin on names. They'll pick up the pattern and try their own names while waiting for the program to begin.

Riddles

What's in a Name? A Book of Name Jokes, **by Jill L. Donahue. Illustrated by Zachary Trover. Picture Window Books, 2007.**

Scatter these name riddles throughout the program. Here are a few examples:

What do you call a woman who gives her stuff to other people?
Sharon.

What do you call a man who always cuts himself shaving?
Nick.

Picture Book

Four Boys Named Jordan, **by Jessica Harper. Illustrated by Tara Calahan King. Putnam, 2004.**

Imagine a classroom that contains four boys all named Jordan. Elizabeth, the narrator, is a bit upset by this fact. It makes life in the classroom very complicated. For example, it's hard to keep them straight. When the teacher asks if Jordan is present, roll call is a mess. When someone asks Jordan to pass the scissors, "you'll end up with four pairs." When a new girl joins the class, Elizabeth sadly acknowledges that her name is Jordan.

Picture Book

Catalina Magdalena Hoopensteiner Wallendiner Hogan Logan Bogan Was Her Name, **by Tedd Arnold. Scholastic, 2004.**

This book is based on an old nonsensical camp song. We see Catalina Magdalena grow up and notice that there are some peculiar aspects about her. As a baby, she had two hairs on her head—one was black and one was red. She has two holes in her nose—one for her fingers and one for her toes. Catalina Magdalena eventually graduates from high school, gets a job at a fish factory, falls in love, and marries a man named Smith. Arnold adds other variations of her name in the back matter along with a score of the song. This is a fun text to sing or read. You can find the melody from Dr. Jean's version of the song, "Patalina Matalina," from her recordings *Dr. Jean and Friends* (Jean Feldman, 1998) and also *Dr. Jean Sings Silly Songs* (Jean Feldman, n.d.). You may even want to write out Catalina Magdalena's full name on a long scroll of paper or a writing board and have the older kids and adults sing it with you during each chorus.

Song

"Lisa Lee Elizabeth." From *Imagine That,* by Monty Harper. Monty Harper Productions, 1996.

This is one of the few instances where I play a fairly long song for a mixed-age audience and they simply sit and listen to the lyrics. However, the young ones will laugh at the silly names, while the older folks will appreciate the absurdity of a girl whose full name is just as silly as Catalina Magdalena's. Here's a sample lyric:

> Mr. and Mrs. McGill,
> they had a daughter, and when they got her,
> all their relations and friends
> wanted to name her after each other.
>
> Aunts and uncles, moms and dads, even the neighbor's dog
> all had names to give the child that they insisted on!
>
> So Mr. and Mrs. McGill
> took their suggestions into the study,
> and after a week they came out
> with an announcement for everybody.
>
> They named her . . .
> Lisa Lee Elizabeth Amanda Francis Jill
> Georgette Suzette Luette Edwina Gina Terry Tina Wilamina
> Mindy Cindy Lauren Wendy Sandra Donna Lil
> Michelle Druzella Ariella Stella Shishkebab
> McGill.

Lisa goes on to college where she meets a boy with the name:

> Tom Paul John Bartholomew Alfonzo Ricky Shane
> Moe Mickey Larry Barry Barney Jerry Terry Eric Duane
> Beau Derrick Melvin Milton Maximillian Zachariah Kane
> Joe William Eddie Teddie Fred Spaghetti Sheldon Eldon
> Payne.

The two get married (the lines the preacher has to say are hilarious), and they have twins. After much deliberation, "They named the twins . . . Mike and Sarah

Payne." You can see the complete lyrics on Harper's website: www.montyharper .com.

Picture Book

My Name Is Yoon, **by Helen Recorvits. Illustrated by Gabi Swiatkowska. Farrar, Straus & Giroux, 2003.**

Yoon moves to American from Korea. Her name in Korean means "Shining Wisdom." Yoon is slow to adjust to her new school and her new language. She stubbornly writes new English words in place of her name on her papers: *cat, bird, cupcake.* When she makes a new friend and realizes her teacher likes her, she proudly writes *Yoon.*

Picture Book

Matthew A.B.C., **by Peter Catalanotto. Atheneum, 2002.**

This is my all-time favorite alphabet book, and it's because the different Matthews represented sometimes border on the absurd. Mrs. Tuttle has twenty-five children (all boys, can you imagine?), and they are all named Matthew. Each Matthew has a character trait that begins with a different letter of the alphabet. Matthew A is extremely affectionate and can be seen constantly hugging his teacher. Matthew B has Band-Aids all over his body. Matthew C has cowlicks that spell out different words. The adults in the audience will be particularly amused by some of the Matthews' outrageous traits, such as Matthew F, who has a cat on his face, and Matthew J, who works a night job (and is seen napping in grease-stained overalls with rags and wrenches in his pockets). Of course, the class gets a new Matthew at the end of the book—Matthew Z, with all of his zippers.

Chant

"Yon Yonson," traditional.

Say this rhyme a few times until people start to roll their eyes.

> My name is Yon Yonson,
> I come from Wisconsin,
> I verk in der lumberyard dere.
> Ven I come down the street,
> All de people I meet say,
> "What's your name?"
> Und I say,
> "My name is Yon Yonson,

I come from Wisconsin,

I verk in der lumberyard dere . . ."

Picture Book

No, David! **by David Shannon. Scholastic, 1998.**

This book became an instant hit when it was published. David's name is shouted several times by his mother. "No, David!" "David! Be quiet!" "Not in the house, David!" Each statement is accompanied by an illustration of David doing something naughty. By the end of the book, David's mother assures him that she still loves him.

Art Activity

No, David! **Scenes**

Supply the kids and their parents with paper, crayons, and markers. Ask them to brainstorm some incidents in their own house where a parent might have said "No!" to their child and draw the scene. Encourage them to include the child's name in the picture. This should be a lighthearted exercise, so ask them to think of fairly silly situations. Encourage them to think of and draw situations that might show the parents saying "Yes!" with big smiles on their faces. As the family members work together, play Jessica Harper's rendition of her song "Four Boys Named Jordan" to make a nice bookend to the program. This song can be found on Harper's recording *Inside Out* (Rounder Records, 2001).

MIX AND MATCH

Additional Picture Books

Addy, Sharon Hart. *Lucky Jake.* **Illustrated by Wade Zahares. Houghton Mifflin, 2007.**

Jake and his father pan for gold. Jake wants a dog but finds a pig instead. He names the pig Dog. Good luck follows them. Dog pulls on Pa's coat, and Jake discovers a seed corn. He plants the seed and raises corn. Dog helps catch a critter chewing the corn. It's a goat. Now they have milk to go with their corn fritters. Prospectors bring items to trade for the corn and milk. They open a restaurant and consider themselves lucky.

Capucilli, Alyssa Satin. *Meet Biscuit.* **HarperCollins, 1998.**

A little girl gets a brand-new puppy. She thinks hard for the perfect name for her new pet. The dog keeps finding a box of dog biscuits. And of course, that's what his name becomes—Biscuit.

Choi, Yangsook. *The Name Jar.* **Knopf, 2001.**

Unhei and her family move to America from Korea. She realizes that her classmates have trouble pronouncing her name. She wants to fit in and find a new name. Her family and friends love her name, which means "grace." Unhei's classmates start a name jar, adding suggestions for new names on slips of paper. One classmate hides the jar because he wants her to keep her real name.

Colato Laínez, René. *I Am René, the Boy: Soy René, el niño.* **Illustrated by Fabiola Graullera Ramírez. Piñata Books, 2005.**

René is upset to learn that his name is a girl's name in the United States. "In El Salvador, I was René the brave, René the strong and René the funny." His desk partner is a girl named Renee. René writes a prizewinning essay about his name that includes a list of famous men named René throughout history.

Jenkins, Emily. *Daffodil.* **Illustrated by Tomek Bogacki. Farrar, Straus & Giroux, 2004.**

Daffodil, Violet, and Rose are identical sisters. Violet gets a pretty violet dress. Rose's dress is pink. Daffodil's dress is yellow. She hates the color of the dress, which corresponds with her name. People called her Dandelion instead of Daffodil. The other girls confess they hate their dresses. In the end, Daffodil wears cherry red pants with a matching jacket.

Keller, Holly. *Nosy Rosie.* **Greenwillow, 2006.**

Rosie helps everyone find lost items with her sniffing talent. However, when she receives the nickname "Nosy Rosie," she becomes angry and refuses to help. Baby Harry goes missing, and Rosie's family realizes how much they need her. She returns with Harry and informs everyone politely to call her Rosie. "And nobody ever called her anything else again."

Additional Songs

"Everybody Has a Name." From *Little Ears: Songs for Reading Readiness,* by Fran Avni. Leapfrog School House, 2000.

"I Had a Friend." From *Buzz Buzz,* by Laurie Berkner. Two Tomatoes, 1998.

"My Name Game." From *Jack in the Box 2,* by Jack Grunsky. Casablanca Kids, 2001.

"My Name Is . . ." From *Underwater,* by Miss Amy. Ionian Productions, 2004.

"The Name Song." From *Ralph's World,* by Ralph's World. Mini Fresh, 2001.

"Tappy Tappy." From *Literacy in Motion,* by the Learning Station. Monopoli/Learning Station, 2005.

Outrageous Hats and Sensible Shoes

PROGRAM AT A GLANCE

Opening Song: "Boots" from *Victor Vito* by Laurie Berkner
Picture Book: *Virginnie's Hat* by Dori Chaconas
Picture Book: *Belinda in Paris* by Amy Young
Song: "My Shoe It Has Three Corners," traditional; adapted by Rob Reid
Picture Book: *Smelly Socks* by Robert Munsch
Song: "Tina's Socks," traditional; adapted by Rob Reid
Picture Book: *Twelve Hats for Lena: A Book of Months* by Karen Katz
Picture Book: *Where's My Sock?* by Joyce Dunbar
Movement Activity: "Serious Sock Hunt"
Picture Book: *Hetty's 100 Hats* by Janet Slingsby
Craft Activity: "Newspaper Hats"

PREPARATION AND PRESENTATION

Opening Song

"Boots." From *Victor Vito*, by Laurie Berkner. Two Tomatoes, 1999.

Everyone will feel like stomping as they enter the story program area and hear singer Laurie Berkner go on about her black boots, brown boots, frog boots, dancing boots, and rain boots. Berkner is one of the more visible children's performers of the past decade, appearing on many television shows.

Picture Book

Virginnie's Hat, by Dori Chaconas. Illustrated by Holly Meade. Candlewick, 2007.

A gust of wind blows a young girl's wide-brimmed hat into the swamp. Virginnie finds the hat high in a tree. She throws a boot at it just as a crawdaddy starts to pinch her toes. The boot misses the hat but falls on the crawdaddy. Virginnie throws her other boot at the hat just as a snake heads for her toes. The boot lands on the snake and it slinks away. Virginnie throws both of her boots at the hat. A gator sneaks up on the girl. The hat falls and Virginnie shrieks, "Yee-haw!" The noise hurts the gator's ears and he leaves. Virginnie's mother finds her and scolds her for being in the swamp full of wild critters. Virginnie replies, "I didn't see a thing!"

Picture Book

Belinda in Paris, by Amy Young. Viking, 2005.

Belinda the Ballerina is performing in Paris. The city is abuzz. Unfortunately, Belinda's special shoes went to Pago Pago instead. Belinda can't wear any type of ballet shoes. Her feet are extraordinarily large. None of the specialty shoe stores in Paris has a pair of shoes large enough for Belinda. The cobbler doesn't have enough fabric. A series of events help Belinda find a special fabric and an even more special "form" so the cobbler can make the shoes in time for the performance.

Song

"My Shoe It Has Three Corners," traditional; adapted by Rob Reid.

In the book *Family Storytime,* I mention that the traditional song "My Hat It Has Three Corners" is tailor-made for multigenerational audiences because it's too tricky for young children to do alone. This time around, I changed the words from *hat* to *shoe.* It's still nonsensical. Instruct the audience to point to themselves each time the word *my* shows up in the lyrics. They point to their feet on *shoes,* hold up three fingers on *three,* and point to their elbows on *corners.* Sing it once with all of the motions.

> *My shoe* it has *three corners,*
> *Three corners* has *my shoe.*
> And had it not *three corners,*
> It would not be *my shoe.*

Sing it a second time, leaving out the word *my.* The audience members still point to themselves. Sing it a third time, leaving out *my* and *shoe,* still doing the motions for those words. Sing it again, dropping the words *my, shoe,* and *three,* complete with motions and then one last time, dropping the previous words plus the word *corners.* The audience may very well give up and giggle, but that's all right.

Picture Book

Smelly Socks, by Robert Munsch. Illustrated by Michael Martchenko. Scholastic, 2004.

Tina and her grandfather row across the river to buy socks. "At the store, Tina tried out socks that were too big, socks that were too little, socks that were too blue, and socks that were too pink." She finds a pair of red, yellow, and green socks. She loves them so much, she never takes them off. They start to stink. The kids in school complain, and wild animals pass out. Her friends throw her in the river, but the stink of the socks chases out the beavers. However, the socks become clean. Tina next wants to go to town to buy a red, yellow, and green shirt.

Song

"Tina's Socks," traditional; adapted by Rob Reid.

Sing to the tune of "Black Socks," simply changing "black socks" to "Tina's socks" and a few pronouns for this perfect follow-up song to Munsch's picture book. Teach the audience to sing it in a round. A version of "Black Socks" sung in a round can be found on Bill Harley's recording *Monsters in the Bathroom* (Round River Records, 1984).

> Tina's socks, they never get dirty,
> The longer she wears them, the stronger they get.
> Sometimes, I think she should wash them,
> But something inside her keeps saying not yet, not yet, not yet, not yet.

Picture Book

Twelve Hats for Lena: A Book of Months, by Karen Katz. McElderry, 2002.

Lena makes a hat for each month of the year. January's hat has tiny snowmen on top. February's hat has a Valentine's Day theme. Have the audience guess what features each month's hat might have before turning the page. March has shamrocks and robins, April has an Easter theme, May has gardening tools and flowers, and so on. December's hat is a challenge for Lena. She wants to highlight Hanukkah, Kwanzaa, and Christmas all on one hat. A large foldout page shows how she accomplishes this. A simple hat craft pattern can be found in the back of the book.

Picture Book

Where's My Sock? by Joyce Dunbar. Illustrated by Sanja Rescek. Scholastic, 2006.

Pippin is angry because he can't find his other yellow sock with the clocks. Tog helps him look. They search the entire house without luck, even finding some socks in the fruit basket. But no yellow sock with clocks. They up the ante by going "on a serious sock hunt." They place their treasures on the clothesline and match them up. The missing sock shows up on Tog's foot.

Movement Activity

"Serious Sock Hunt"

Follow up Dunbar's picture book with a sock hunt of your own. Before the program begins, gather several colorful pairs of socks, mix them up, and hide the socks throughout the story program area or corresponding space. Hang up a clothesline in the area. Ask the children in the audience to find and match the socks. Parents can help locate any hard-to-reach spots. As the children return with the socks, place them on the clothesline. Another possibility is to make several pairs of colorful felt socks and hide those. These can be placed on a felt board as they are found.

Picture Book

Hetty's 100 Hats, by Janet Slingsby. Illustrated by Emma Dodd. Good Books, 2005.

Hetty starts out with three hats to wear during the different seasons. When she picks up a few more hats, she becomes interested in collecting one hundred hats. She even invents some hats out of household items, like the colander. Soon, various family members, people in the community, classmates, and friends help Hetty build her collection. Her last hat is a newspaper hat. Instructions for making a newspaper hat are included in the book.

Craft Activity

"Newspaper Hats"

Bring several newspapers and Scotch tape to the program. Follow the directions in the back of *Hetty's 100 Hats*. Several of the family members in the audience are probably old pros at making newspaper hats. Have audience members wear their hats proudly as they leave the story program area.

MIX AND MATCH

Additional Picture Books

Daly, Niki. *Happy Birthday, Jamela!* **Farrar, Straus & Giroux, 2006.**

Jamela goes shopping for birthday clothes and shoes. She wants to buy the Princess Shoes, but her mother makes her take a pair of black school shoes. Once home, Jamela decorates the black shoes with glue, glitter, and beads. Mama is angry. Jamela runs into the artist neighbor who loves the decorated shoes. Together, the two make and sell several pairs of "Jamela Shoes" at the market. Jamela makes enough money to buy the Princess Shoes.

Dunbar, Joyce. *Shoe Baby.* **Illustrated by Polly Dunbar. Candlewick, 2005.**

A baby hides in a shoe and has a series of adventures with sea creatures, zoo animals, birds, and royalty. The baby takes a nap and dreams about a giant who walks around with one shoe and a crying giantess. The giant is the baby's father looking for his shoe. The giantess is the baby's mother worried about the baby. The baby jumps out of the shoe shouting, "Peekaboo!" Throughout the story, the baby says, "How do you do?" Have the audience say this with the baby.

Light, Steve. *The Shoemaker Extraordinaire.* **Abrams, 2003.**

Hans Crispin is a traveling shoemaker. He shows up at a village and creates shoes that match each unique wearer. He makes tall shoes for a short man, shoes that make a girl the center of attention, and a fisherman special boat shoes. A jealous cobbler tricks Hans Crispin into going into the giant Barefootus's cave. The giant plans on eating Hans Crispin, but the shoemaker quickly makes special shoes for Barefootus. The two become friends and teach the evil cobbler a lesson.

Mitchell, Marianne. *Joe Cinders.* **Illustrated by Bryan Langdo. Holt, 2002.**

A poor cowboy named Joe Cinders is forced to labor for his three lazy stepbrothers in this Cinderella parody. Miss Rosalinda sends an invitation to the fall fiesta. The three evil stepbrothers "take their once-a-year baths" and dress up as robbers. An old man shows up and magically helps Joe turn into a well-dressed cowboy complete with red boots. At the ball, Joe dances with Miss Rosalinda and then runs away, leaving behind one boot. Of course, it fits Joe, and the two get married. They live at the Red Boot Dude Ranch, where the stepbrothers have "important" jobs.

Ross, Tony. *Centipede's 100 Shoes.* **Holt, 2002.**

A little centipede goes to the shoe store and buys one hundred new shoes— the lace-up type. It takes a long time for the little centipede to put the shoes on.

His shoes hurt his feet so the little centipede has to put on one hundred pairs of socks. The centipede decides it's not worth the bother and gives the shoes and socks to "friends with fewer legs."

Rumford, James. *Don't Touch My Hat!* Knopf, 2007.

Sheriff John is in charge of law and order in the little town of Sunshine. He's very proud of his ten-gallon hat as he gathers up the bad guys. He's always telling others, including his wife, "Don't touch my hat!" One night, Sheriff John gets a call and runs out of the house wearing one of his wife's hats. The audience will enjoy seeing the illustrations of Sheriff John arresting rustlers in a fancy woman's hat full of flowers and streamers. The book is fairly didactic with its message, "It's your heart, not your hat," but works if read in the style of an old-time western.

Additional Songs

"I Can't Find My Shoes." From *Big Rock Rooster,* by Daddy A Go Go. Boyd's Tone, 2002.

"I Got a Hat." From *Seasonal Songs in Motion,* by the Learning Station. Monopoli/Learning Station, 2001.

"I Love My Little Hat." From *Wiggleworms Love You,* by the Old Town School of Folk Music. Old Town School, 2005.

"New Shoes." From *Good Kid,* by Peter and Ellen Allard. Peter and Ellen Allard, 2000.

"Tall Silk Hat." From *Music Is Magic,* by Magical Music Express. Magical Music Express, 2002.

"Walkin' Shoes." From *Look at My Belly,* by Brady Rymer. Bumblin' Bee, 2002.

Papas, Granddads, and Uncles

PROGRAM AT A GLANCE

Opening Song: "Dads Who Rock" from *Eat Every Bean and Pea on Your Plate* by
     Daddy A Go Go
Picture Book: *Daddy Mountain* by Jules Feiffer
Picture Book: *Minnie's Diner* by Dayle Ann Dodds
Poem: "Fraidy Cat" by Matthew F. Fredericks from *Rolling in the Aisles: A
     Collection of Laugh-Out-Loud Poems*
Movement Activity: "Bubble Gum," traditional
Picture Book: *Yo, Jo!* by Rachel Isadora
Movement Activity: "My Grand Old Uncle York," traditional
Picture Book: *What Uncles Do Best/What Aunts Do Best* by Laura Joffe Numeroff
Picture Book: *My Father the Dog* by Elizabeth Bluemle
Movement Activity: "Father Abraham," traditional

PREPARATION AND PRESENTATION

Opening Song

**"Dads Who Rock." From *Eat Every Bean and Pea on Your Plate*, by Daddy A
Go Go. Boyd's Tone, 2006.**

What father will not grin ear to ear when he hears this rock-and-roll song
upon entering the story program area? Daddy A Go Go not only sings about dads
doing the boogie-woogie but moms, too, who like to dance to the beat. Daddy A
Go Go is John Boydston, who left the journalism field to raise his kids and sing
rock and roll for other people's kids.

Picture Book

Daddy Mountain, **by Jules Feiffer. Hyperion, 2004.**

A little girl climbs up her father's legs as if she were mountain climbing. Have fun reading the first-person voice as she "struggles" to his belt and then his shirt. "Remember, the Daddy Mountain must wear a shirt. Because if you grab his skin, he'll get mad." She makes it onto his shoulders and, finally, the top of his head. One page folds out vertically to show how great her accomplishment was.

Picture Book

Minnie's Diner, **by Dayle Ann Dodds. Illustrated by John Manders. Candlewick, 2004.**

Papa McFay warns his five sons that "there'll be no eatin' till your work is through." The smells from Minnie's Diner draw the boys from their work one by one. The littlest brother orders "1 soup, 1 salad, 1 sandwich, some fries, and 1 of her special hot cherry pies." As the bigger brothers appear in the diner, their meal orders grow bigger and bigger. Papa McFay, who has been unseen at this point, is upset that the boys all left their work. When he opens the door to the diner, we realize Papa McFay is tiny, but that he casts an enormous shadow. On his way out, Papa McFay catches a whiff of the pies and orders double.

Poem

"Fraidy Cat," by Matthew F. Fredericks. From *Rolling in the Aisles: A Collection of Laugh-Out-Loud Poems,* **edited by Bruce Lansky. Meadowbrook, 2004.**

The narrator states that "he" is afraid of monsters and cries. The kids check the closets and behind the doors for "him." The punch line is that "he" is Dad.

Movement Activity

"Bubble Gum," traditional.

Teach the chorus of this camp chant favorite to the audience members and have them wave their hands overhead while they say "Ba-umpa-umpa bubble gum."

> My granddad gave me a penny
> And told me to buy some Good and Plenty.
> But I didn't buy Good and Plenty.
> Instead I bought some bubble gum!
>
> Chorus: Ba-umpa-umpa bubble gum,
> Ba-umpa-umpa bubble gum.

My granddad gave me a nickel
And told me to buy to buy a pickle.
But I didn't buy a pickle.
Instead I bought some bubble gum!

Ba-umpa-umpa bubble gum,
Ba-umpa-umpa bubble gum.

My granddad gave me a dime
And told me to buy a lime.
But I didn't buy a lime.
Instead I bought some bubble gum!

Ba-umpa-umpa bubble gum,
Ba-umpa-umpa bubble gum.

My granddad gave me a quarter
And told me to buy some water.
But I didn't buy some water.
Instead I bought some bubble gum!

Ba-umpa-umpa bubble gum,
Ba-umpa-umpa bubble gum.

My granddad gave me a dollar
And told me to buy a collar.
But I didn't buy a collar.
Instead I bought some bubble gum!

Ba-umpa-umpa bubble gum,
Ba-umpa-umpa bubble gum.

My granddad gave me a large sum
And told me to buy some bubble gum.
And so . . .
I bought some bubble gum!

Ba-umpa-umpa bubble gum,

Ba-umpa-umpa bubble gum.

Picture Book

Yo, Jo! by Rachel Isadora. Harcourt, 2007.

Franklin and his brother Jomar wait for their grandpa to come down the street. While they wait, they are greeted by others with slang phrases, such as "S'up, Jomar," "Off the heazy," and the title phrase. When Jomar greets his grandfather with, "Yo! Chillin'," Grandpa looks puzzled. Jomar next says, "I love you, Grandpa," to which Grandpa says, "That's better." Grandpa then greets Franklin with, "Yo, Franklin, you chillin' with us?"

Movement Activity

"My Grand Old Uncle York," traditional.

All I did was change "The Grand Old Duke of York" to "My Grand Old Uncle York" to fit the program theme.

My Grand Old Uncle York

He had ten thousand men.

He marched them up a hill.   *(everyone stand)*

He marched them down again.   *(everyone sit)*

And when you're up, you're up.   *(everyone stand)*

And when you're down, you're down.   *(everyone sit)*

But when you're only halfway up   *(stand and lean forward)*

You're neither up   *(stand all the way up)*

Nor down.   *(sit)*

Rarely do I get an audience where the adults willingly stand and sit throughout the entire activity. Tell them it's OK to raise and lower their hands instead of getting up and down. That way, they are still participating.

Picture Book

What Uncles Do Best/What Aunts Do Best, **by Laura Joffe Numeroff. Illustrated by Lynne Munsinger. Simon & Schuster, 2004.**

The book is designed to flip halfway through. One side tells all of the things uncles can do, such as buy you cotton candy, make triple-decker sandwiches, tell jokes, and go for rides. Flip the book and read about aunts. They can do a lot of the same things as uncles. Other books in the series include *What Mommies Do Best/What Daddies Do Best* (Simon & Schuster, 1998) and *What Grandpas Do Best/What Grandmas Do Best* (Simon & Schuster, 2000).

Picture Book

My Father the Dog, by Elizabeth Bluemle. Illustrated by Randy Cecil. Candlewick, 2006.

A child has a theory that her father is really a dog. He starts the day by scratching. He fetches the paper, he likes to roughhouse, he lies around for hours, he chases a ball, and he investigates noises. "Mom says we can keep him." All ages will be particularly amused by the fact that "when he toots, he looks around the room like someone else did it."

Movement Activity

"Father Abraham," traditional.

End the program with another camp favorite. Ask everyone to stand.

Father Abraham had seven sons, seven sons had Father Abraham.
They never laughed.   *(laugh "ha, ha")*
They never cried.   *(cry "boo hoo")*
All they did was go like this:
Left arm!   *(wave left arm)*

Father Abraham had seven sons, seven sons had Father Abraham.
They never laughed.   *(laugh "ha, ha")*
They never cried.   *(cry "boo hoo")*
All they did was go like this:
Left arm!   *(wave left arm)*
Right arm!   *(wave right arm)*

Father Abraham had seven sons, seven sons had Father Abraham.
They never laughed.   *(laugh "ha, ha")*
They never cried.   *(cry "boo hoo")*
All they did was go like this:
Left arm!   *(wave left arm)*
Right arm!   *(wave right arm)*
Both hips!   *(swing both hips)*

Father Abraham had seven sons, seven sons had Father Abraham.
They never laughed.   *(laugh "ha, ha")*
They never cried.   *(cry "boo hoo")*
All they did was go like this:
Left arm!   *(wave left arm)*
Right arm!   *(wave right arm)*
Both hips!   *(swing both hips)*
Turn around!   *(turn in a circle)*

Make up your own orders and motions. If you include this activity earlier in a program, add the command "Sit down!" at the very end.

MIX AND MATCH

Additional Picture Books

Grindley, Sally. *No Trouble at All.* **Illustrated by Eleanor Taylor. Bloomsbury, 2002.**

A grandfather bear takes care of his little bear cubs for the evening. He's convinced that they are good little bears. The illustrations show, in fact, that the bears are up to mischief. The bear cubs stay one step ahead of the grandpa bear, who concludes that the cubs deserve a treat for being "no trouble at all."

Leuck, Laura. *I Love My Pirate Papa.* **Illustrated by Kayle M. Stone. Harcourt, 2007.**

A young boy loves it when his pirate father takes him out on the pirate ship. They dig for buried treasure and join the pirate belching contest. Papa puts the child to bed and says that of all the treasure he has found, "there's nothing I prize more than you, my dearest pirate boy."

London, Jonathan. *Froggy's Day with Dad.* **Illustrated by Frank Remkiewicz. Viking, 2004.**

Froggy helps make breakfast for Father's Day. He makes a mess, but Froggy's dad is a good sport. "The eggshells are nice and crunchy." The two go to the batting cage, ride the bumper boats, and go miniature golfing. The book contains London's trademark sound effects the audience can repeat.

Quigly, Mary. *Granddad's Fishing Buddy.* **Illustrated by Stéphane Jorisch. Dial, 2007.**

A little girl convinces her grandfather that she's old enough to go fishing with him. She keeps her eyes open for Granddad's fishing buddy. The friend turns out to be a wild heron that shows Granddad where the fish are hiding. The two catch a lot of fish, and the granddaughter becomes Granddad's new fishing buddy.

Rex, Michael. *You Can Do Anything, Daddy!* **Putnam, 2007.**

A father assures his son that he will always be there for him. Even if it means saving his son from regular pirates, gorilla pirates, robot gorilla pirates, and even robot gorilla pirates from Mars. The child, in turn, promises to give his daddy a drink of water and kiss his bruises for all of his troubles.

Willems, Mo. *Knuffle Bunny.* **Hyperion, 2004.**

Trixie accompanies her father to the Laundromat. They put the clothes in the washer and head out when Trixie realizes that her stuffed rabbit, Knuffle Bunny, is missing. She tries to tell her dad, but he doesn't understand baby talk. It's not until they reach home and Mommy asks about Knuffle Bunny that the father catches on. They all race back to the Laundromat and retrieve Knuffle Bunny. I usually point out the man in the book who wears a pigeon shirt, based on the author's popular Pigeon books. I then tell the audience that Willems sells the Pigeon shirts on his website, www.mowillems.com, and that they make great gifts for children's literature enthusiasts (hint, hint).

Ziefert, Harriet. *Bigger Than Daddy.* **Illustrated by Elliot Kreloff. Blue Apple, 2006.**

Edward wants to be as tall as a tree and as fast as a truck. His father assures Edward that he will grow big in a few years. They pretend that Edward is big and Daddy is little. Daddy refuses to make dinner because "I'm too little to fix dinner." They switch back to their proper roles before Daddy tucks Edward in bed.

Additional Songs

"Dads Can Dance." From *Blast Off!* by Ben Rudnick. Ben Rudnick, 2004.

"Grandpa Says." From *Mojo A Go Go,* by Daddy A Go Go. Boyd's Tone, 2004.

"I Caught Daddy Watching Cartoons." From *Big Rock Rooster,* by Daddy A Go Go. Boyd's Tone, 2002.

"My Dad's a Jungle Gym." From *Uh-Oh!* by Peter Alsop. Moose School, 2002.

"My Dad's the Greatest." From *Good Kid,* by Peter and Ellen Allard. Peter and Ellen Allard, 2000.

"We're on Our Way." From *Marvelous Day!* by SteveSongs. Rounder Records, 2006.

Super Moms, Super Grandmas, and Super Aunts

PROGRAM AT A GLANCE

Opening Song: "Going to Grandma's" from *Little Red Wagon* by Timmy Abell
Picture Book: *That's What Grandmas Are For* by Harriet Ziefert
Picture Book: *Here Comes Grandma!* by Janet Lord
Song: "My Grandmother Had a House," traditional; adapted by Rob Reid
Picture Book: *My Granny Went to Market: A Round-the-World Counting Rhyme*
    by Stella Blackstone
Movement Activity: "The New My Aunt Came Back," traditional; adapted by
    Rob Reid
Picture Book: *Mommies Say Shhh!* by Patricia Polacco
Picture Book/Felt Board: *If Mom Had Three Arms* by Karen Kaufman Orloff
Movement Activity: "Mommy, Mommy," author unknown

PREPARATION AND PRESENTATION

Opening Song

"Going to Grandma's." From *Little Red Wagon*, by Timmy Abell. Upstream, 2005.
    The catchy chorus will attract the attention of audience members as they
settle down for the program. "I'm goin' to see my Grandma! Sure is a long, long
way." Abell sings about traveling by car, subway, bus, plane, and more. The lyrics
are available on Abell's website: www.timmyabell.com.

Picture Book

That's What Grandmas Are For, **by Harriet Ziefert. Illustrated by Amanda Haley. Blue Apple, 2006.**

There are several picture books on the market that describe the nice qualities of grandmothers. This book is unique because the point of view shifts at midpoint, and Grandmother extols the wonders of grandchildren. Grandmas are special because "If I tell my grandma I want to run away from home, she will suggest a sleep-over at her house." Grandchildren are wonderful because "If I think I've learned pretty much everything worth knowing, I listen to my grandchildren and learn that there is always more to know."

Picture Book

Here Comes Grandma! **by Janet Lord. Illustrated by Julie Paschkis. Holt, 2005.**

Grandma travels in a variety of modes of transportation. She starts on a bicycle. Have everyone in the audience make the noise of a bicycle bell. She leaps on a horse and clip-clops. Have the audience slap their legs for the horse's clip-clop. The audience can also make the sounds of the car, the train, the skis ("swish, swish"), the hot air balloon ("whoosh"), and the airplane that Grandma rides. She also races a submarine underwater, so have everyone make swimming motions while saying "Glub, glub." At the end, Grandma gives her grandchild a great big hug. The audience members can hug themselves or each other.

Song

"My Grandmother Had a House," traditional; adapted by Rob Reid.

Sing this ditty to the tune of "Old MacDonald." My family and I had fun coming up with the noisy items in Grandmother's house. We didn't have to look far. My wife and I learned that we were going to be grandparents for the first time while I was working on this chapter.

> My grandmother had a house, E-I-E-I-O.
> And in this house, she had a clock, E-I-E-I-O.
> With a tick-tock here and a tick-tock there,
> Here a tick, there a tock, everywhere a tick-tock,
> My grandmother had a house, E-I-E-I-O.

My grandmother had a house, E-I-E-I-O.
And in this house, she had a teapot, E-I-E-I-O.
With a *(whistle)* here and a *(whistle)* there,
Here a *(whistle)*, there a *(whistle)*, everywhere a *(whistle)*,
A tick-tock here and a tick-tock there,
Here a tick, there a tock, everywhere a tick-tock,
My grandmother had a house, E-I-E-I-O.

My grandmother had a house, E-I-E-I-O.
And in this house, she had a rocking chair, E-I-E-I-O.
With a squeak-squeak here and a squeak-squeak there,
Here a squeak, there a squeak, everywhere a squeak-squeak,
A *(whistle)* here and a *(whistle)* there,
Here a *(whistle)*, there a *(whistle)*, everywhere a *(whistle)*,
A tick-tock here and a tick-tock there,
Here a tick, there a tock, everywhere a tick-tock,
My grandmother had a house, E-I-E-I-O.

My grandmother had a house, E-I-E-I-O.
And in this house, she had a grandpa, E-E-I-O.
With a *(snore)* here and a *(snore)* there,
Here a *(snore)*, there a *(snore)*, everywhere a *(snore)*,
A squeak-squeak here and a squeak-squeak there,
Here a squeak, there a squeak, everywhere a squeak-squeak,
A *(whistle)* here and a *(whistle)* there,
Here a *(whistle)*, there a *(whistle)*, everywhere a *(whistle)*,
A tick-tock here and a tick-tock there,
Here a tick, there a tock, everywhere a tick-tock,
My grandmother had a house, E-I-E-I-O.

Picture Book

My Granny Went to Market: A Round-the-World Counting Rhyme, by Stella
Blackstone. Illustrated by Christopher Corr. Barefoot Books, 2005.
   Granny buys a flying carpet in Istanbul and flies all over the world to purchase
other items. She buys two cats in Thailand, three masks in Mexico, four paper
lanterns in China, five cowbells in Switzerland, six drums in Kenya, seven nesting

dolls in Russia, eight boomerangs in Australia, nine kites in Japan, and ten llamas in Peru. The book's endpapers show Granny's travels on a world map. You may want to place a large world map on the wall and pin paper flying carpets to all of the places that Granny visited.

Movement Activity

"The New My Aunt Came Back," traditional; adapted by Rob Reid.

   The traditional "My Aunt Came Back," which can be found in *Family Storytime,* is, without a doubt, of all of the movement activities I use with kids and adults, the one that gets the biggest response. This new version was created in the same spirit. I had a blast coming up with countries and rhyming activities. It's a call-and-response activity where the participants add the new motions while still performing the old motions.

   Well, my aunt came back (Well, my aunt came back)
   From Old Belize,   (From Old Belize,)
   She had some fun   (She had some fun)
   In the gentle breeze.   (In the gentle breeze.)
   (Participants raise their hands overhead and sway.)

   Well, my aunt came back   (Well, my aunt came back)
   From fine old France,   (From fine old France,)
   She got worn out   (She got worn out)
   From doing a dance.   (From doing a dance.)
   (Participants dance in place while swaying arms overhead.)

   Well, my aunt came back   (Well, my aunt came back)
   From Ecuador,   (From Ecuador,)
   She got caught up   (She got caught up)
   Inna revolving door.   (Inna revolving door.)
   (Spin while dancing in place and swaying arms overhead.)

   Well, my aunt came back   (Well, my aunt came back)
   From Cameroon,   (From Cameroon,)
   She got caught in   (She got caught in)
   A big typhoon.   (A big typhoon.)
   (Blow with gusto while spinning and dancing in place and swaying arms overhead.)

Well, my aunt came back   (Well, my aunt came back)
From Italy,   (From Italy,)
She hurried home   (She hurried home)
'Cuz she missed me!   ('Cuz she missed me!)
(Stop all motions and point to self.)

Picture Book

Mommies Say Shhh! **by Patricia Polacco. Philomel, 2005.**

The audience can make several bird and animal sound effects throughout the book. Birds cheep, squirrels say "chee, chee, chee," dogs say "buff," sheep baa, geese honk, chickens cluck, ducks quack, goats say "ma-a-a," cows moo, cats meow, pigs oink, and horses neigh. The refrain is "bunnies say nothing at all." Prep the audience beforehand and tell them to make bunny ears with their fingers and wiggle their noses when they hear this line. The book ends with "Mommies say shhh, shhh, shhh," and the illustrations show a sleeping baby. Whisper the last lines.

Picture Book/Felt Board

If Mom Had Three Arms, **by Karen Kaufman Orloff. Illustrated by Pete Whitehead. Sterling, 2006.**

A grocery-bag-carrying mom says, "I only have two arms" when her son asks her to carry his backpack. He imagines what his mom would be like with more arms. With three arms she could be a circus act. With four arms she could direct traffic coming from all directions. And so on through twenty arms where, as president, she is shaking hands and talking to several people on the phones at once. Two arms work the best for hugging. Make a large felt woman and add the many arms to this felt character as you read the story.

Movement Activity

"Mommy, Mommy," author unknown.

I found this on several early childhood websites. Have everyone stand for this closing activity.

Mommy, mommy, let's sweep the floor.   *(mime sweeping the floor)*
Mommy, mommy, let's go to the store.   *(mime turning a steering wheel)*
Mommy, mommy, let's bake a cake.   *(mime mixing ingredients)*
Mommy, mommy, let's take a break.   *(wipe brow and say "Whew")*

Mommy, mommy, loves me so. *(point to heart)*

Mommy, mommy, watch me grow. *(stretch arms up high)*

Mommy, mommy, turn out the light. *(make a click sound and turn pretend light off)*

Mommy, mommy, say "Good night." *(place head in hands)*

MIX AND MATCH

Additional Picture Books

Edwards, Pamela Duncan. *Rosie's Roses.* **Illustrated by Henry Cole. HarperCollins, 2003.**

Rosie the Raccoon tries to deliver four roses for her aunt Ruth's birthday. Along the way, she loses the orange rose to Mr. Rat, the purple rose to Mr. Rabbit, and the red rose to the robins. She gladly gives the white rose to a squirrel bride who "forgot to make a garland for my hair." Rosie only has the rainbow ribbon that held the roses left. Aunt Ruth proudly declares she already has a prize rose—her niece Rosie.

Lindbergh, Reeve. *My Hippie Grandmother.* **Illustrated by Abby Carter. Candlewick, 2003.**

Grandmother hasn't cut her hair "since nineteen sixty-nine." She drives a purple bus and has a cat named Woodstock and a fish named Tiny Tim. Her house is full of plants and posters that say "LOVE" and "FLOWER POWER!" They visit the Farmer's Market, picket City Hall, and sing songs in the evening. Grandmother tells the narrator, who falls asleep on psychedelic sheets, that she can be anything she wants.

Odanaka, Barbara. *Skateboard Mom.* **Illustrated by JoAnn Adinolfi. Putnam, 2004.**

A boy gets a new skateboard for this birthday. Before he can use it, his mother gets a gleam in her eye and takes the skateboard out for a spin. It turns out that Mom was a champion skateboarder who not only rode a skateboard to the senior prom but also to her wedding. The boy gets a second skateboard and asks his mother to teach him to skate. Before they can ride off together, Granny gets a gleam in *her* eye.

Prigger, Mary Skillings. *Aunt Minnie and the Twister.* **Illustrated by Betsy Lewin. Clarion, 2002.**

Minnie lives in rural Kansas with her nine orphaned nieces and nephews. She clangs her bell when she needs to get their attention. The kids all pitch in to help with the chores. A storm hits one spring day. Minnie shakes her bell. They all cling to each other and make it to the cellar before the twister hits. They are amazed to find that the farmhouse is intact but turned completely around.

Ziefert, Harriet. *41 Uses for a Grandma.* **Illustrated by Amanda Haley. Blue Apple, 2005.**

Ziefert has a long list of words that describe the functions of grandmothers. Number one is that grandmothers serve as security blankets. They also make great lounge chairs, hair braiders, e-pals, movie companions, pillows, pet sitters, and friends. Other books in this series include *39 Uses for a Friend* (Putnam, 2001), *31 Uses for a Mom* (Putnam, 2003), *33 Uses for a Dad* (Blue Apple, 2004), and *40 Uses for a Grandpa* (Blue Apple, 2004).

Additional Songs

"Grandma's House Tonight." From *Take Me to Your Library,* by Monty Harper. Monty Harper, 2003.

"Grandma's Video Camera." From *Spinning Tails,* by Steve Pullara. Cool Beans, 2001.

"My Awesome Mom." From *Martian Television Invasion,* by Thaddeus Rex. Thaddeus Rex, 2005.

"My Grandma and Me." From *Sing and Dance,* by Jack Grunsky. Casablanca Kids, 2000.

"My Mother's Snoring." From *The Lost Songs of Kenland,* by Ken Lonnquist. Kenland, 1998.

"No One Loves You More Than Your M-O-Double M-Y." From *Singin' in the Bathtub,* by John Lithgow. Sony, 1999.

The Tricksters

PROGRAM AT A GLANCE

Opening Song: "Stone Soup" from *Magic Parade* by Elizabeth McMahon
Picture Book: *Smart Feller Fart Smeller, and Other Spoonerisms* by Jon Agee
Picture Book: *Love and Roast Chicken: A Trickster Tale from the Andes Mountains*
    by Barbara Knutson
Poem: "One Winter Night in August" from *Exploding Gravy: Poems to Make You*
    Laugh by X. J. Kennedy
Activity: "Boom-Chicka-Boom," traditional
Picture Book: *Oink?* by Margie Palatini
Musical Activity: "John Brown's Baby," traditional
Picture Book: *Just a Minute: A Trickster Tale and Counting Book* by Yuyi Morales
Musical Activity: "My Bonnie Lies over the Ocean," traditional
Picture Book: *Whoo? Whoo?* by David A. Carter

PREPARATION AND PRESENTATION

Opening Song

"Stone Soup." From *Magic Parade*, by Elizabeth McMahon. Mrs. McPuppet, 2006.

    McMahon puts a musical spin on this classic trickster tale that involves the cooperation of neighbors to make stone soup. Audience members will start singing the catchy chorus as they wait for the program to begin. McMahon is the best children's performer when it comes to writing original songs adapted from classic folktales.

Picture Book

Smart Feller Fart Smeller, and Other Spoonerisms, **by Jon Agee. Hyperion, 2006.**

Spoonerisms are a form of wordplay where the initial sounds of words are switched around. Scatter Agee's twenty-eight spoonerisms throughout the program. These are set up as riddles. Read the spoonerisms and see if the audience can figure out what the real phrase is supposed to be. An answer key is located in the back of the book. Examples include "You have very mad banners" for "You have very bad manners" and "You need to shake a tower" for "You need to take a shower."

Picture Book

Love and Roast Chicken: A Trickster Tale from the Andes Mountains, **by Barbara Knutson. Carolrhoda, 2004.**

Cuy, a guinea pig, outwits Tio Antonio, a fox, over and over in this hilarious story. Cuy first convinces Tio Antonio to hold up a rock so the sky doesn't fall. Cuy next traps Tio Antonio in a den, convincing the fox that the world is burning. Cuy's luck runs out when a farmer catches him stealing alfalfa. Cuy tricks the fox to take his place, promising him the love of the farmer's daughter and a plate of the farmer's chickens every day. Knutson's version was developed from traditional sources. Read the book, or try telling it as an oral tale without the book.

Poem

"One Winter Night in August: How Many Things Are Wrong with This Story?" From *Exploding Gravy: Poems to Make You Laugh,* by X. J. Kennedy. Little, Brown, 2002.

Take note of the subtitle of this poem. Read it slowly and ask the audience to comment on the misstatements. Examples include "But then with an awful holler / That didn't make a peep, / Our ancient boy (age seven) / Woke up and went to sleep."

Activity

"Boom-Chicka-Boom," traditional.

I learned this one from some of my students who worked as camp counselors. Challenge the audience to repeat everything you say with this tricky chant.

> I said a boom-chicka-boom!   (I said a boom-chicka-boom!)
>
> I said a boom-chicka-boom!   (I said a boom-chicka-boom!)
>
> I said a boom-a-chicka-rocka-chicka-rocka-chicka-boom!   (I said a boom-a-chicka-rocka-chicka-rocka-chicka-boom!)

Uh-huh,   (Uh-huh,)
Oh, yeah,   (Oh, yeah,)
This time   (This time)
We sing   (We sing)
Higher!   (Higher!)

Repeat the above call-and-response ditty in a falsetto voice. Add other verses in the following styles: lower, in a whisper, louder, slower, faster, underwater style (move finger on lips while chanting), and opera style (grandiose singing styles). There are several variations of this camp favorite on the Internet.

Picture Book

Oink? by Margie Palatini. Illustrated by Henry Cole. Simon & Schuster, 2006.

Thomas and Joseph are two lazy but content pigs. The other barnyard occupants are disgusted by the pigs. The hens insist the pigs whitewash their fence. The pigs do a lousy job of it, so the hens finish the project. The rabbit insists the pigs gather fresh vegetables. The pigs wreck the garden, so the rabbit gathers the produce herself. The duck wants the pigs to dig a water hole for cleanliness. The pigs have bad shoveling techniques, so the duck digs the hole and drags the pails of water. By the end of the book, the hens, rabbit, and duck wonder if the pigs aren't "as dumb as we thought they were." Adults will recognize elements of Mark Twain's *The Adventures of Tom Sawyer* in this book.

Musical Activity

"John Brown's Baby," traditional.

I remember this tricky challenge from my own days at camp. Sing it to the tune of "The Battle Hymn of the Republic." Sing it once to teach the audience. Then inform the audience that every time they sing it again, they are going to substitute motions for words. Challenge them to keep up with you.

John Brown's baby had a cold upon his chest,
John Brown's baby had a cold upon his chest,
John Brown's baby had a cold upon his chest,
And they rubbed it with camphorated oil.

John Brown's *(make rocking motions with arms)* had a cold upon his chest,
John Brown's *(rock arms)* had a cold upon his chest,
John Brown's *(rock arms)* had a cold upon his chest,
And they rubbed it with camphorated oil.

John Brown's *(rock arms)* had a *(sneeze)* upon his chest,
John Brown's *(rock arms)* had a *(sneeze)* upon his chest,
John Brown's *(rock arms)* had a *(sneeze)* upon his chest,
And they rubbed it with camphorated oil.

John Brown's *(rock arms)* had a *(sneeze)* upon his *(pound chest)*,
John Brown's *(rock arms)* had a *(sneeze)* upon his *(pound chest)*,
John Brown's *(rock arms)* had a *(sneeze)* upon his *(pound chest)*,
And they rubbed it with camphorated oil.

John Brown's *(rock arms)* had a *(sneeze)* upon his *(pound chest)*,
John Brown's *(rock arms)* had a *(sneeze)* upon his *(pound chest)*,
John Brown's *(rock arms)* had a *(sneeze)* upon his *(pound chest)*,
And they *(rub chest)* it with camphorated oil.

John Brown's *(rock arms)* had a *(sneeze)* upon his *(pound chest)*,
John Brown's *(rock arms)* had a *(sneeze)* upon his *(pound chest)*,
John Brown's *(rock arms)* had a *(sneeze)* upon his *(pound chest)*,
And they *(rub chest)* it with *(hold nose)*.

Picture Book

***Just a Minute: A Trickster Tale and Counting Book,* by Yuyi Morales. Chronicle, 2003.**

Señor Calavera (*calavera* means "skull" in Spanish) tells Grandma Beetle that it's her time to go. She says, "Just a minute, Señor Calavera." She needs to sweep one house. Señor Calavera waits. When she's done, Grandma Beetle says, "Just a minute, Señor Calavera." She needs to boil two pots of tea. And so it goes. Every time Señor Calavera is ready to take Grandma Beetle away, she asks for another minute. We learn she is preparing for a birthday party with her nine grandchildren. Number ten is their guest, Señor Calavera. He doesn't take Grandma Beetle with him after all. Have the audience repeat Grandma Beetle's lines, "Just a minute, Señor Calavera" as well as the English and Spanish numbers that pepper the text.

Musical Activity

"My Bonnie Lies over the Ocean," traditional.

Here's another tricky camp song designed to keep the audience alert. Lead everyone singing the traditional song "My Bonnie Lies over the Ocean." Instruct them to alternate from sitting positions to standing positions on each word in the song that begins with the letter *B*. Sing it twice, the first time slowly to let everyone practice. Then speed it up.

My *Bonnie* lies over the ocean,

My *Bonnie* lies over the sea,

My *Bonnie* lies over the ocean,

Oh, *bring back* my *Bonnie* to me.

Bring back, bring back, oh, *bring back* my *Bonnie* to me, to me.

Bring back, bring back, oh, *bring back* my *Bonnie* to me.

Picture Book

Whoo? Whoo? by David A. Carter. Simon & Schuster, 2007.

Let audience members catch their breath from the last activity to guess what Carter's tiny shapes represent. The first page has a question mark and a series of triangles, ovals, and other shapes. Turn the page and see that the shapes make a lamb. The kids can make the sounds of the animals to end the program.

MIX AND MATCH

Additional Picture Books

Aylesworth, Jim. *The Tale of Tricky Fox*. Illustrated by Barbara McClintock. Scholastic, 2001.

Tricky Fox makes a bet that he can fool a human into putting a fat pig into a sack for him. He tricks a kindly old lady into giving him a loaf of bread and a chicken. When he goes back a third time to trick her into giving him a pig, she outwits the fox by putting a bulldog in the sack. "But Tricky Fox hadn't counted on one important thing, and that was that this particular lady was a teacher. And Tricky Fox didn't know that teachers are not so easy to fool as regular humans are."

Bateman, Teresa. *Traveling Tom and the Leprechaun*. Illustrated by Mélisande Potter. Holiday House, 2007.

The king's daughter tells all that the man she'll marry must be clever enough to "win a leprechaun's pot of gold in a single day's time." Tom learns about this and devises a plan to trick a leprechaun. By the end of his adventure, the leprechaun is begging Tom to take the pot of gold.

Campoy, F. Isabel. *Rosa Raposa*. Illustrated by Joe Aruego and Ariane Dewey. Harcourt, 2002.

Rosa the fox outwits Jaguar in a series of adventures. In one story, Jaguar is trapped in a hole. He gets away, but Rosa tricks him into entering the trap once again. The highlight is the story where Rosa tricks Jaguar into getting tied to a tree so as to not be blown away by the wind.

Kimmel, Eric. *Anansi and the Magic Stick.* **Illustrated by Janet Stevens. Holiday House, 2001.**

Anansi the lazy trickster steals Hyena's magic stick. Anansi uses the stick to do his chores for him. Anansi falls asleep while the magic stick waters the vegetables, and the stick makes a flood that carries all of the animals away. Hyena comes to the rescue and retrieves his magic stick. The book ends with Anansi "planning new tricks, which is just what Anansi does best." Look for pictures of the author and illustrator in the flood scene.

Lexau, Joan M. *Crocodile and Hen.* **Illustrated by Doug Cushman. HarperCollins, 2001.**

Crocodile is about to eat Hen, but her quick thinking saves her life. She calls Crocodile "My brother" in midbite. He snaps shut his mouth, watches her walk away, and ponders her comment. He asks Lizard how he can be brother to Hen. Lizard convinces Crocodile that what Hen says is true. This simple, dialogue-heavy text is good for a puppet show.

Rand, Gloria. *Little Flower.* **Illustrated by R. W. Alley. Holt, 2002.**

Miss Pearl taught Little Flower, her pet potbellied pig, how to roll over and play dead. The neighbors have mixed reactions to this trick. Little Flower knows that she can attract attention with her trick. One day, Miss Pearl has an accident in the house. Little Flower rushes outside and plays dead. However, no one pays any attention. Rescue finally arrives when Little Flower plays dead in the middle of the street.

Willans, Tom. *Wait! I Want to Tell You a Story.* **Simon & Schuster, 2004.**

A muskrat outwits a hungry tiger by telling a long, strung-out story. The story involves a frog tricking a shark, a lizard tricking a snake, and a fly trying to trick a spider. However, the spider succeeds in eating the fly. The spider, in turn, is eaten by the lizard. All of the characters in the story are eaten by other characters. This long story stalls the tiger long enough for a crocodile to sneak up and save the muskrat.

Additional Songs

"Little Anancy," by Asheba. From *Caribbean Playground.* Putumayo, 2004.

"Stone Soup." From *Don't Kiss a Codfish/When I Grow Up,* by Tom Knight. Tom Knight, 2005.

"Too Much Noise." From *Magic Parade,* by Elizabeth McMahon. Mrs. McPuppet, 2006.

Uh-Oh! Accidents!

PROGRAM AT A GLANCE

Opening Song: "Scabs" from *Ooey Gooey* by Jim Cosgrove
Picture Book: *Chickens to the Rescue* by John Himmelman
Poem: "Oops" from *Kindergarten Kids: Riddles, Rebuses, Wiggles, Giggles, and More* by Stephanie Calmenson
Movement Activity: "Ow, Ow, I Bumped My Head" by Rob Reid
Picture Book: *Terrific* by Jon Agee
Movement Activity: "Jack and Jill," traditional
Picture Book: *17 Things I'm Not Allowed to Do Anymore* by Jenny Offill
Musical Activity: "Let Everyone Clap Hands," traditional
Picture Book: *Please Don't Upset P. U. Zorilla!* by Lynn Rowe Reed

PREPARATION AND PRESENTATION

Opening Song

"Scabs." From *Ooey Gooey*, by Jim Cosgrove. Hiccup, 2001.
The tone for this story program will be immediately apparent when family members hear Cosgrove chanting "scabs, scabs, scabs, scabs, scabs . . ." The song describes what appears on bodies as the result of accidents. Cosgrove, also known as "Mr. Stinky Feet," has performed his songs with the Kansas City Symphony.

Picture Book

***Chickens to the Rescue,* by John Himmelman. Holt, 2006.**

This hilarious picture book will have several opportunities for the audience to yell "Chickens to the rescue" at the top of their voices. Farmer Greenstalk (I can already hear the adults chuckle at his name) loses his watch. Turn the page. "Chickens to the rescue!" A flock of chickens, complete with swimming suits, bathing caps, and snorkels, dives into the well and retrieves the watch. The chickens heroically appear to help other members of the Greenstalk family when accidents happen.

Poem

"Oops." From *Kindergarten Kids: Riddles, Rebuses, Wiggles, Giggles, and More,* by Stephanie Calmenson. HarperCollins, 2005.

Different folks have small accidents during the school day. Anna breaks her crayon, and Michael overwaters the avocado tree. The music teacher misses a note, and "Our principal said, 'Good morning,' / When it was afternoon." The ending verse states that it's OK to make mistakes.

Movement Activity

"Ow, Ow, I Bumped My Head," by Rob Reid.

Have everyone repeat the progressive lines and perform the motions.

Ow, ow, I bumped my head!   (Ow, ow, I bumped my head!)
(Hold head.)

Ow, ow, I squashed my nose and bumped my head!   (Ow, ow, I squashed my nose and bumped my head!)
(Hold nose, then head.)

Ow, ow, I hurt my tummy and squashed my nose and bumped my head! (Ow, ow, I hurt my tummy and squashed my nose and bumped my head!)
(Add motion of holding tummy.)

Ow, ow, I landed on my seat and hurt my tummy and squashed my nose and bumped my head!   (Ow, ow, I landed on my seat and hurt my tummy and squashed my nose and bumped my head!)
(Sit and then do the rest of the motions.)

Ow, ow, I skinned my knee and landed on my seat and hurt my tummy and squashed my nose and bumped my head!   (Ow, ow, I skinned my knee and landed on my seat and hurt my tummy and squashed my nose and bumped my head!)

(Hold knees, then sit and do the rest of the motions.)

Ow, ow, I stubbed my toe and skinned my knee and landed on my
seat and hurt my tummy and squashed my nose and bumped my
head!   (Ow, ow, I stubbed my toe and skinned my knee and landed
on my seat and hurt my tummy and squashed my nose and bumped
my head!)

(Grab toe and hop around, hold knee, then sit and do the rest of the motions.)

I need a kiss!   (I need a kiss!)

(Make kissing noises.)

All better!   (All better!)

(Big smile.)

Picture Book

Terrific, by Jon Agee. Hyperion, 2005.

Pessimist Eugene wins a cruise to Bermuda. He grumps, "I'll probably get
a really nasty sunburn." The ship sinks, and Eugene is the only passenger not
rescued. He gets washed up on a tiny island. "'Terrific,' he said. 'Now I'll get
eaten by cannibals.'" A parrot is also stranded on the island and, despite Eugene's
attitude, instructs Eugene how to build a boat to get them off the island. They are
rescued by the parrot's rightful owners, but the parrot decides to stay with crabby
Eugene, who replies, "Terrific," without a hint of sarcasm.

Movement Activity

"Jack and Jill," traditional.

Jack and Jill went up the hill   *(lift feet and hands as if walking up a steep hill)*
To fetch a pail of water.
Jack fell down   *(sit down)*
And broke his crown,   *(hold head)*
And Jill came tumbling after.   *(twirl hands)*

Repeat two more times, each time slightly faster.

Picture Book

17 Things I'm Not Allowed to Do Anymore, by Jenny Offill. Illustrated by
Nancy Carpenter. Schwartz & Wade, 2007.

This book features naughty activities instead of accidents, but a case can be
made for the protagonist's "intentional" accidents. "I had an idea to staple my

brother's hair to his pillow. I'm not allowed to use the stapler anymore" is just the first of many naughty incidents a young girl commits. She also glues her brother's bunny slippers to the floor, walks backward to school, freezes a dead fly in an ice cube, flings cauliflower at her brother, pretends her mother is a waitress and complains about the food, and shows "Joey Whipple my underpants."

Musical Activity

"Let Everyone Clap Hands," traditional.

I added commentary between lines of this traditional song to fit the theme. The melody can be found on the recording *Wee Sing in the Car* (Price Stern Sloan, 1999).

> Let everyone clap hands like me.   *(clap, clap)*
> Let everyone clap hands like me.   *(clap, clap)*
> Come on and join in the game,
> You'll find that it's always the same.   *(clap, clap)*
>
> Spoken: What happens when something bad happens?
> Let everyone cry like me.   (Boo hoo)
> Let everyone cry like me.   (Boo hoo)
> Come on and join in the game,
> You'll find that it's always the same.   (Boo hoo)
>
> Spoken: What happens when you get sick?
> Let everyone sneeze like me.   (Ah-choo)
> Let everyone sneeze like me.   (Ah-choo)
> Come on and join in the game,
> You'll find that it's always the same.   (Ah-choo)
>
> Spoken: What happens when your hiccups don't stop?
> Let everyone hiccup like me.   (Hic hic)
> Let everyone hiccup like me.   (Hic hic)
> Come on and join in the game,
> You'll find that it's always the same.   (Hic hic)
>
> Spoken: What do you do at the end of a bad day?
> Let everyone sleep like me.   *(snore)*
> Let everyone sleep like me.   *(snore)*

Come on and join in the game,
You'll find that it's always the same. *(snore)*

Spoken: Tomorrow's going to be a better day!
Let everyone clap hands like me. *(clap, clap)*
Let everyone clap hands like me. *(clap, clap)*
Come on and join in the game,
You'll find that it's always the same. *(clap, clap)*

Picture Book

Please Don't Upset P. U. Zorilla! **by Lynn Rowe Reed. Knopf, 2006.**

Mayor Tootlebee tries his best to find a job for a skunk named P. U. Zorilla. The skunk gets a job driving the school bus until the children's arguing upsets P. U. He lets loose with "a gush of skunk spray." The mayor finds the skunk more jobs, each time pleading with everyone, "Please don't upset P. U. Zorilla." However, accidents happen, and the skunk lets its spray loose. P. U. gets one last chance—cleaning the mayor's wife's store. A bad man robs the store. P. U. tries not to get upset, but he cracks under pressure. He sprays the robber and saves the day. The mayor changes the name of the town to Stinkville and makes P. U. the chief of police. Have the audience contribute hissing noises whenever P. U. sprays.

MIX AND MATCH

Additional Picture Books

Derby, Sally. *The Wacky Substitute*. Illustrated by Jennifer Herbert. Marshall Cavendish, 2005.

Mr. Wuerst's glasses slipped into the frying pan and shattered. The phone rings, and he picks up a banana. He finally finds the phone and accepts a substituting job for the local kindergarten. He accidentally frees the twelve gerbils because he thinks they are fur caps. He gives the kids the wrong treat and reads the wrong story. He falls asleep at rest time, and the kids restore order to their room. At the end of the day, Mr. Wuerst tells everyone he's going to see the eye doctor, and he walks into the girls' bathroom.

Fox, Mem. *A Particular Cow*. Illustrated by Terry Denton. Harcourt, 2006.

A cow goes on a walk. "Usually nothing particular happens." This particular Saturday, the cow runs into a string of accidents. A pair of bloomers covers the cow's eyes, and she falls on the postman's cart. It rolls down a hill and scatters dogs, children, and a wedding party. The cow lands on a boat in the middle of the river, hops onto land, and "went on her way without surprise."

Freedman, Claire. *Oops-a-Daisy!* Illustrated by Gaby Hansen. Tiger Tales, 2004.

A small rabbit tries to hop all by herself. She loses her balance and falls time after time. Mama Rabbit shows Daisy that the other young animals are having accidents while learning new skills. Little Mouse falls down. Little Badger's tunnel collapses. Little Duckling swims in circles. Daisy persists and becomes a good hopper.

Johnson, Adrian. *That's Not Funny!* Bloomsbury, 2005.

Alfie laughs when bad things happen to other people. He laughs when a dog chases the mailman, a guard at Buckingham Palace trips, a jogger hits a tree, and a window cleaner gets a tourist wet. When a circus elephant falls on Alfie, the boy yells, "That's not funny!" The book's back matter discusses the German word *schadenfreude,* defined as "a malicious delight in the bad luck of others."

Shannon, David. *David Gets in Trouble.* Scholastic, 2002.

David pleads that it was an accident whenever he gets into trouble. He breaks the window with a baseball, he has an excuse for not turning in his homework, he makes faces for the class picture, he pulls the cat's tail, he drops his purple drink all over the floor, and he belches loud enough to cause the candle to flame higher and the flowers to bend over. He does apologize in the end.

Wardlow, Lee. *The Chair Where Bear Sits.* Illustrated by Russell Benfanti. Winslow, 2001.

A series of small pages mixed with large glossy pages tell a "This Is the House That Jack Built" cumulative type of story. We see a chair, a tray, a bowl with oatmeal, a spoon, some juice, a dog, a cat, a dad, a mom, a baby, a teddy bear, and a flying insect—all participants in a chain of events that leads to a household accident.

Willems, Mo. *Knuffle Bunny, Too: A Case of Mistaken Identity.* Hyperion, 2007.

Trixie takes her "one-of-a-kind Knuffle Bunny" to school. She's dismayed to find out that Sonja also has a Knuffle Bunny. The two even argue about how to pronounce *Knuffle,* which librarians and teachers will appreciate. The bunnies get mixed up, but Trixie doesn't realize the mishap until the middle of the night. Her father and Sonja's father meet for the exchange.

Additional Songs

"The Boo Boo Song." From *Do You Wish You Could Fly?* by Kathy Byers. KT Music, 2000.

"Boo Boo Waltz." From *Touched by a Song,* by Miss Jackie Silberg. Miss Jackie Music, 2004.

"My Name Is Burt." From *Blast Off!* by Ben Rudnick. Ben Rudnick, 2004.

"Oops Oops Bang Bang." From *A Poodle in Paris,* by Connie Kaldor. Folle Avoine, 2004.

Under the Deep Blue Sea, Sea, Sea

PROGRAM AT A GLANCE

Opening Song: "Out on the Beach" from *Take Me to Your Library* by Monty Harper
Picture Book: *I'm the Biggest Thing in the Ocean* by Kevin Sherry
String Story: "The Sardines" from *String Stories: A Creative Hands-On Approach for Engaging Children in Literature* by Belinda Holbrook
Fingerplay: "Five Little Fishies," traditional
Picture Book: *The Three Little Fish and the Big Bad Shark* by Ken Geist
Musical Activity: "She Waded in the Ocean," traditional
Picture Book: *Five Little Sharks Swimming in the Sea* by Steve Metzger
Movement Activity: "Have You Ever Gone Fishing?" traditional

PREPARATION AND PRESENTATION

Opening Song

"Out on the Beach." From *Take Me to Your Library*, by Monty Harper. Monty Harper, 2003.

Oklahoma musician Harper recalls going to a California beach with his mother and his father—a memory that's perfect for a family storytime. Play it as people enter the story program area. Have an assortment of beach towels around for families to sit on.

Picture Book

***I'm the Biggest Thing in the Ocean,* by Kevin Sherry. Dial, 2007.**

The blue giant squid that takes up much of the double-page spreads of this oversize picture book brags about his size. We see the squid in comparison to shrimp, clams, a crab, a jellyfish, turtles, an octopus, a shark, and "this fish, that fish, this fish, and that fish." The giant squid doesn't look so big once a whale appears. The whale swallows the stunned giant squid, who finds himself in the whale's stomach with other sea creatures. He quickly regains his composure, however, and proudly states, "I'm the biggest thing in this whale!"

String Story

"The Sardines." From *String Stories: A Creative Hands-On Approach for Engaging Children in Literature,* by Belinda Holbrook. Linsworth, 2002.

This resource book has several string stories that work well for a variety of family story program themes. "The Sardines," which is based on a folktale about a fisherman, is one of the easier stories to learn. The fisherman sees two sardines in his net but waits for a bigger catch. More and more fish get caught. Before the man hauls the net in, two big fish swim by and eat up all of the sardines. The poor fisherman goes home with an empty net.

Fingerplay

"Five Little Fishies," traditional.

The audience can perform this while sitting.

Five little fishies were swimming in a pool.   *(wiggle five fingers)*

The first little fish said, "This pool is cool."   *(hold up one finger, shiver, and hug self)*

The second little fish said, "This pool is deep."   *(hold up two fingers and say "deep" with a deep voice)*

The third little fish said, "I want to sleep."   *(hold up three fingers, then put head on hands)*

The fourth little fish said, "Let's take a dip."   *(hold up four fingers, then place hands together as if diving)*

The fifth little fish said, "I see a ship!"   *(hold up five fingers, then shade eyes with hand as if looking far away)*

A fishing boat comes and a line goes splash,   *(mime throwing a fishing line)*

And the five little fishies swim away in a dash!   *(wiggle five fingers behind back quickly)*

Picture Book

The Three Little Fish and the Big Bad Shark, **by Ken Geist. Illustrated by Julia Gorton. Scholastic, 2007.**

Three fish, named Jim, Tim, and Kim, swim off "to make a home in the deep blue sea." Jim makes a house out of seaweed, Tim makes a house out of sand, and Kim settles in a sunken wooden ship. The big bad shark appears at Jim's house and states, "Little fish, little fish, let me come in." Jim replies, "Not by the skin of my finny fin fin." The shark then says, "I'll munch and I'll crunch and I'll smash your house in." Teach these lines to your audience before the story begins so they can recite them throughout this underwater version of "The Three Pigs."

Musical Activity

"She Waded in the Ocean," traditional.

Sing this camp favorite to the tune of "The Battle Hymn of the Republic." Have everyone stand and point and wiggle the various body parts as they are mentioned in the song. The audience will quickly learn the clapping parts.

> She waded in the ocean and she got her feet all wet.
> She waded in the ocean and she got her feet all wet.
> She waded in the ocean and she got her feet all wet.
> But she didn't get her *(clap, clap)* wet *(clap)* yet.

> Glory, Glory, Hallelujah!
> Glory, Glory, Hallelujah!
> Glory, Glory, Hallelujah!
> But she didn't get her *(clap, clap)* wet *(clap)* yet.

> She waded in the ocean and she got her ankles wet.
> She waded in the ocean and she got her ankles wet.
> She waded in the ocean and she got her ankles wet.
> But she didn't get her *(clap, clap)* wet *(clap)* yet.

> Glory, Glory, Hallelujah!
> Glory, Glory, Hallelujah!
> Glory, Glory, Hallelujah!
> But she didn't get her *(clap, clap)* wet *(clap)* yet.

> She waded in the ocean and she got her knees all wet.
> She waded in the ocean and she got her knees all wet.

She waded in the ocean and she got her knees all wet.
But she didn't get her *(clap, clap)* wet *(clap)* yet.

Glory, Glory, Hallelujah!
Glory, Glory, Hallelujah!
Glory, Glory, Hallelujah!
But she didn't get her *(clap, clap)* wet *(clap)* yet.

She waded in the ocean and she got her swimsuit wet. *(wiggle whole body)*
She waded in the ocean and she got her swimsuit wet.
She waded in the ocean and she got her swimsuit wet.
Yes, she finally got her bathing suit wet! *(lead everyone clapping several times)*

Picture Book

Five Little Sharks Swimming in the Sea, **by Steve Metzger. Illustrated by Laura Bryant. Scholastic, 2005.**

Read this oceanic version of "Five Little Monkeys Jumping on the Bed" that features five little sharks facing mishaps one by one. The first little shark bumps into a manatee, the second shark gets stuck on the ocean floor, the third shark bangs into a whale, the fourth shark gets lost, and the last shark overeats. Each time, the mother shark calls the doctor. Have your audience make the following hand gestures while you read: hold up the corresponding number of fingers to represent the sharks. Move your fingers back and forth as if they were sharks swimming. Mime using a telephone when mother shark calls the doctor and wag a finger when the doctor replies. The audience members can also bump their fingers into their other hand for the first and third shark, place their finger on the floor for the second shark, look around and shrug their shoulders for the fourth shark, and hold their stomachs and make a face for the fifth shark.

Movement Activity

"Have You Ever Gone Fishing?" traditional.

Have everyone stand for this closing routine.

Have you ever gone fishing on a bright and sunny day,   *(mime casting a fishing line)*
When all the little fish are swimming in and out of the bay?   *(make swimming motions)*

With their hands in their pockets,   *(place hands in front pockets of pants
    or on front of legs)*

And their pockets in their pants,   *(place hands in back pockets of pants or
    on backside)*

All the fishes do the hoochie-koochie dance.   *(everyone dance)*

MIX AND MATCH

Additional Picture Books

Berkes, Marianne. *Over in the Ocean in a Coral Reef.* **Illustrated by Jeanette
Canyon. Dawn Publications, 2006.**

Many adults know the traditional song "Over in the Meadow." Sing the same
tune to the text of this picture book. Many of the adults will join in for the baby
fishes' lines. "Over in the ocean far away from the sun, / Lived a mother octopus
and her octopus one, / 'Squirt,' said the mother, / 'I squirt,' said the one, / So
they squirted in the reef far away from the sun." Other lines feature parrot fish,
clown fish, stingrays, puffer fish, dolphins, angelfish, needlefish, grunt fish, and
sea horses. Score and chords are included.

Carle, Eric. *Mister Seahorse.* **Philomel, 2004.**

As Mister Seahorse takes care of his eggs, he encounters other fish species
where fathers care for the eggs and babies. These include the stickleback, the
tilapia, the kurtis, the pipefish, and the bullhead. Painted transparent pages also
hide trumpet fish, a lionfish, leaf fish, and a stonefish.

Galloway, Ruth. *Smiley Shark.* **Tiger Tales, 2003.**

Smiley Shark loves to smile. He's "the friendliest and funniest, the biggest and
toothiest of all the fish." Unfortunately, the other fish see those large teeth and
swim away. The reader gets a quick glimpse of an angelfish, a puffer, a starfish, a
jellyfish, an octopus, and a catfish before they flee from Smiley Shark. The shark
saves the fish from a fishnet, and they all become friends.

Peck, Jan. *Way Down Deep in the Deep Blue Sea.* **Illustrated by Valerie
Petrone. Simon & Schuster, 2004.**

A little boy goes diving into the ocean. He meets a sea horse, a hermit crab,
a starfish, a sea turtle, an octopus, a dolphin, a swordfish, a whale, and a shark.
He also discovers a treasure chest. After each encounter, the audience can say the
refrain, "Swim away." The boy finally surfaces, and we see that he is in his bathtub,
and the sea creatures are bath toys. This would be a good cumulative story to use
with felt characters. Patterns can be found on several "coloring pages" sites on the
Internet.

Wood, Audrey. *The Deep Blue Sea.* **Illustrated by Bruce Wood. Scholastic, 2005.**
    The story begins with the deep blue sea and adds a red rock, green tree, brown nut, purple parrot, orange butterfly, black spot, yellow sun, and white cloud. The cloud turns dark, and rain falls on "the rock in the middle of the sea."

Additional Songs

"At the Bottom of the Sea." From *At the Bottom of the Sea,* by Ralph's World. Mini Fresh, 2002.

"The Beach Song." From *Music Is Magic,* by Magical Music Express. Magical Music Express, 2002.

"Goin' to the Coral Reef." From *Splash Zone,* by Linda Arnold. Youngheart Records, 2000.

"Home on the Sea." From *Singing Science,* by Tickle Tune Typhoon. Music for Little People, 2000.

"So Happy under the Sea." From *I Love Toy Trains,* by James Coffey. Blue Vision Music, 2005.

"Woo-Woo." From *Bottle of Sunshine,* by Milkshake. Milkshake, 2004.

What'cha Gonna Wear?

PROGRAM AT A GLANCE

Opening Song: "I Had an Old Overcoat" from *Literacy in Motion* by the
    Learning Station
Picture Book: *Fancy Nancy* by Jane O'Connor
Picture Book: *Five Little Monkeys Go Shopping* by Eileen Christelow
Song: "R-I-N-G-O," traditional; adapted by Jayne Freij
Picture Book: *The Spiffiest Giant in Town* by Julia Donaldson
Movement Activity: "If You're Wearing a Shirt" by Rob Reid
Picture Book: *New Clothes for New Year's Day* by Hyun-Joo Bae
Movement Activity: "My Name Is Joe; I Work in a Clothing Factory," traditional;
    adapted by Rob Reid
Picture Book: *Mr. Tanen's Tie Trouble* by Maryann Cocca-Leffler
Art Activity: "Make a New Tie for Mr. Tanen"

PREPARATION AND PRESENTATION

Opening Song

**"I Had an Old Overcoat." From *Literacy in Motion*, by the Learning Station.
Monopoli/Learning Station, 2005.**
    Adults may recognize the traditional plot sung about in the song as they enter
the story program area. The Learning Station was created by Don and Laurie
Monopoli, who share traditional and original music, often matching songs with
specific picture books.

Picture Book

Fancy Nancy, **by Jane O'Connor. Illustrated by Robin Preiss Glasser. HarperCollins, 2006.**

Nancy loves being fancy. Her shoes have sparkles, her sandwiches have frill toothpicks, and her doll's name is Marabella Lavinia Chandelier. Nancy is upset at her family. They are so ordinary. She gives them lessons on being fancy. They accessorize their clothing. They pretend their car is a limousine and they eat with their pinkie fingers up. Nancy trips with the dessert tray and gets messy. "I don't feel fancy anymore." They head back home for homemade sundaes. Nancy realizes that there isn't a fancy way to say "I love you."

Picture Book

Five Little Monkeys Go Shopping, **by Eileen Christelow. Clarion, 2007.**

Mama Monkey takes her five monkeys shopping for school clothes. One by one, the monkeys wander off. In the meantime, other monkey children join her and she has trouble keeping track. At one point, she has ten little monkeys in her care. The audience members can help count aloud with Mama and supply the correct answer before you read Mama's answer.

Song

"R-I-N-G-O," traditional; adapted by Jayne Freij.

Ask the kids if they know anyone famous whose name is Ringo. If the parents don't answer (and they will), tell them about the Beatles drummer and how he used to wear a lot of rings on his fingers. Have everyone hold up five fingers and wiggle them one at a time for each letter sung. Wiggle the thumb for *R,* pointer finger for *I,* middle finger for *N,* ring finger for *G,* and pinkie for *O.* Sing to the traditional song "B-I-N-G-O." Clap legs (to simulate Ringo's drums) for each letters that is dropped.

> There was a drummer had a band and Ringo was his name-o.
> R-I-N-G-O, R-I-N-G-O, R-I-N-G-O,
> And Ringo was his name-o.
>
> There was a drummer had a band and Ringo was his name-o.
> *(Clap)*-I-N-G-O, *(Clap)*-I-N-G-O, *(Clap)*-I-N-G-O,
> And Ringo was his name-o.
>
> There was a drummer had a band and Ringo was his name-o.
> *(Clap-clap)*-N-G-O, *(Clap-clap)*-N-G-O, *(Clap-clap)*-N-G-O,
> And Ringo was his name-o.

There was a drummer had a band and Ringo was his name-o.
(Clap-clap-clap)-G-O, *(Clap-clap-clap)*-G-O, *(Clap-clap-clap)*-G-O,
And Ringo was his name-o.

There was a drummer had a band and Ringo was his name-o.
(Clap-clap-clap-clap)-O, *(Clap-clap-clap-clap)*-O, *(Clap-clap-clap-
clap)*-O,
And Ringo was his name-o.

There was a drummer had a band and Ringo was his name-o.
(Clap-clap-clap-clap-clap), *(Clap-clap-clap-clap-clap)*, *(Clap-clap-clap-
clap-clap)*,
And Ringo was his name-o.

Picture Book

The Spiffiest Giant in Town, **by Julia Donaldson. Illustrated by Axel Scheffler. Dial, 2002.**

George is a giant. He wears scruffy clothes. He spots a new clothing store and buys some spiffy clothes. He meets a giraffe with a cold neck and gives it his spiffy tie to wear. He also provides his spiffy shirt as a sail for a boat, one spiffy shoe as a house for a family of mice, one spiffy sock as a sleeping bag to a fox, and his spiffy belt to keep a dog from sinking in a bog. He resorts back to wearing his scruffy clothes. However, the animals reward him with a spiffy gold paper crown.

Movement Activity

"If You're Wearing a Shirt," by Rob Reid.

Everyone sits. They stand only if they are wearing the article of clothing mentioned. Then they sit again until the next verse that applies to them. Give them ample time to perform each action.

> If you're wearing a shirt . . . stand and pretend you're digging in the dirt.
> If you're wearing any pants . . . stand and do a little dance.
> If you're wearing a hat . . . stand and meow like a cat.
> If you're wearing a ring . . . stand and let me hear you sing.
> If you're wearing a dress . . . stand and nod your head yes   (the rest of you sit and shake your head no).
> If you're wearing any underwear . . . *(big pause)* . . . That's OK, you just sit there.

Picture Book

New Clothes for New Year's Day, **by Hyun-Joo Bae. Kane/Miller, 2007.**

A Korean girl is happy that it's finally New Year's Day and she can wear her new clothes. We see her put them on one by one. First is her crimson skirt with a white sash. Next are her embroidered socks. These are followed by her rainbow-striped jacket, headband, hair ribbon, flowered shoes, furry vest, winter hat, and a charm and lucky bag on the jacket string.

Movement Activity

"My Name Is Joe; I Work in a Clothing Factory," traditional; adapted by Rob Reid.

Have everyone sit and perform the following movements. I took the traditional camp activity and moved Joe from a button factory to a clothing factory to fit the story program theme.

> Hi. My name is Joe.
> I work in a clothing factory.
> I have a wife and a dog and a family.
> One day my boss said, "Joe, are you busy?" and I said no.
> So he said to test this hat.
> *(Mime lifting a hat up and down off your head with right hand.)*
>
> Hi. My name is Joe.
> I work in a clothing factory.
> I have a wife and a dog and a family.
> One day my boss said, "Joe, are you busy?" and I said no.
> So he said to test these pants.
> *(Move legs back and forth one at a time while continuing the hat motion with right hand.)*
>
> Hi. My name is Joe.
> I work in a clothing factory.
> I have a wife and a dog and a family.
> One day my boss said, "Joe, are you busy?" and I said no.
> So he said to test these gloves.
> *(Spread fingers and close fist over and over with left hand while moving legs and continuing the hat motion with right hand.)*

Hi. My name is Joe.

I work in a clothing factory.

I have a wife and a dog and a family.

One day my boss said, "Joe, are you busy?" and I said no.

So he said to test this belt.

(Swivel waist back and forth while performing the previous motions.)

Hi. My name is Joe.

I work in a clothing factory.

I have a wife and a dog and a family.

One day my boss said, "Joe, are you busy?" and I said YES!

(Yell and stand.)

Picture Book

Mr. Tanen's Tie Trouble, **by Maryann Cocca-Leffler. Whitman, 2003.**

Principal Tanen, the owner of 975 ties, is sad to learn that there's little money for the new playground. He decides to sell his tie collection. The whole town shows up for the auction, and they successfully raise enough money. On opening day, Mr. Tanen is surprised to see his old ties decorating the new playground equipment. The townspeople give him back his old ties.

Art Activity

"Make a New Tie for Mr. Tanen"

Photocopy and distribute coloring sheets with a tie pattern as well as crayons and markers. Remind the audience of the different ties that Mr. Tanen owns. These include his Doughnut and Danish Tie, Back-to-Jail Tie, School Bus Tie, Pizza Tie, Swing and Slide Tie, Book Tie, Toothbrush Tie, Hot Dog Tie, Wedding Bells Tie, Crabapple Tie, and Ribbon-Cutting Tie. Ask the families to brainstorm and draw a new tie for Mr. Tanen. One of my family groups came up with a Skateboard Tie, a Dogsled Race Tie, and a Map of the Hawaiian Islands Tie.

MIX AND MATCH

Additional Picture Books

Lester, Helen. *The Sheep in Wolf's Clothing.* Illustrated by Lynn Munsinger. Houghton Mifflin, 2007.

Ewetopia tries to impress the other sheep at the Woollyone's Costume Ball. She dresses up as a wolf. A crafty wolf shows up dressed as a sheep. He mistakes Ewetopia for his mother. He tells her about his plot to dine on the sheep. Still pretending to be his mother, Ewetopia scolds the wolf and tells him to take a bath, brush his fangs, and pick up his room. The wolf goes into a tantrum and becomes too weary to chase the sheep.

Lloyd, Sam. *What Color Is Your Underwear?* Scholastic, 2003.

Several animals reveal the title question through the book's lift-the-flap format. Harry Horse has cherry red boxers, Tommy Turtle has purple underwear, and Susie Sheep has woolly green bloomers. Sally Spider wears four pairs of lacy, pink underwear, and Elephant isn't wearing any at all.

Sheth, Kashmira. *My Dad Wears a Sari.* Illustrated by Yoshiko Jaeggi. Peachtree, 2007.

Daddima shows her young granddaughter the advantages of wearing saris— even in America, where the rest of the family dresses in skirts, blouses, and pants. She also shares her three favorite saris: her first sari as a little girl, the sari she wore on the plane from India to America, and her wedding sari.

Spinelli, Eileen. *In My New Yellow Shirt.* Illustrated by Hideko Takahashi. Holt, 2001.

A boy proudly shows off his new yellow shirt and compares himself to several yellow objects. "In my new yellow shirt, I am a duck quacking." He also states that he is a lion, a taxi, a caterpillar, a daffodil, a tropical fish, a tennis ball, a trumpet, a canary, and more, ending with the fireflies.

Taback, Simms. *Joseph Had a Little Overcoat.* Viking, 1999.

Taback's Caldecott Award–winning die-cut format features Joseph's overcoat, which is old and worn. He trims it down to make a jacket. When the jacket gets old, Joseph fashions it into a vest. He in turn makes a scarf, necktie, handkerchief, and button out of the material. When the button is lost, Joseph writes a book about it, "which shows you can always make something out of nothing."

Additional Songs

"All Dressed Up." From *Good Kid,* by Peter and Ellen Allard. Peter and Ellen Allard, 2000.

"Bring Your Clothes." From *Whaddaya Think of That?* by Laurie Berkner. Two Tomatoes, 2000.

"Dirty Laundry Boogie." From *Don't Kiss a Codfish/When I Grow Up,* by Tom Knight. Tom Knight, 2005.

"Dress Up Queen." From *Don't Blink,* by Parachute Express. Trio Lane, 2004.

"Fancy Pants Dance." From *Pick Me! Pick Me!* by Jim Cosgrove. Hiccup, 2003.

"Let's Get Dressed." From *Spin Your Web,* by Mary Kaye. Mary Kaye Music, 2006.

What's Cooking?

PROGRAM AT A GLANCE

Opening Song: "Pass the Purple Pesto Pasta Please" from *What's Eatin' Yosi?* by Yosi
Picture Book: *Bad Boys Get a Cookie* by Margie Palatini
Picture Book: *Stone Soup* by Jon J. Muth
Song: "Fruit Round," traditional; adapted by Rob Reid
Picture Book/Props: *Bean Thirteen* by Matthew McElligot
Musical Activity: "Ravioli," traditional
Picture Book: *Yoko* by Rosemary Wells
Picture Book: *A Birthday Cake Is No Ordinary Cake* by Debra Frasier
Craft Activity: "Paper Plate Cake Clock" by Debra Frasier
Party/International: "After-Program International Food Day Party"

PREPARATION AND PRESENTATION

Opening Song

"Pass the Purple Pesto Pasta Please." From *What's Eatin' Yosi?* by Yosi. Yosi, 2006.
Toes will be tapping as family members enter the story program area and encounter Yosi's tongue-twisting, Dixieland-band tune. Yosi grew up in New York City and now performs out of Island Heights, New Jersey.

Picture Book

Bad Boys Get a Cookie! by Margie Palatini. Illustrated by Henry Cole.
HarperCollins, 2006.

The two big bad wolves Willy and Wally chase the runaway cookie (think of the Gingerbread Man) to satisfy their "big bad sweet tooths." The wolves dress up as Hansel and Gretel to lure the cookie, but they fail. They try to trap the cookie in a puddle of honey, but they encounter a skunk. Teach the audience the cookie's refrain: "Na-na-ni-na-na! Lookee! Lookee! You can't get me. I'm one smart cookie!" The cookie finally skips away from the wolves, but it gets snapped up by an alligator. "I believe that little crumb is not as smart as he thinks he is." Still dressed as Hansel and Gretel, the wolves encounter a witch standing in front of her cottage made of sweets. She invites them to eat at her house. "I've got the oven warming right now."

Picture Book

Stone Soup, by Jon J. Muth. Scholastic, 2003.

Three monks enter a village full of suspicious and uncooperative inhabitants. The monks decide to teach them happiness. They do this by making stone soup. A little girl brings the monks three stones and a large pot. The villagers become curious. The monks convince them the soup is good but would be better with a few more ingredients. The villagers bring spices, carrots, onions, mushrooms, and other items. They have a joyous feast. The villagers thank the monks. "You have shown us that sharing makes us all richer."

Song

"Fruit Round," traditional; adapted by Rob Reid.

I found a round online similar to this, kept the line about "bright red apples," and changed the rest. Sing to the tune "Are You Sleeping?" also known as "Frère Jacques." Divide the audience into four groups. Have one group start as soon as the previous group finishes one line.

> Bright red apples, bright red apples,
> Pears and plums, pears and plums,
> Very ripe bananas, very ripe bananas,
> Muskmelon, muskmelon.

Picture Book/Props

Bean Thirteen, by Matthew McElligot. Putnam, 2007.

Two insects pick thirteen beans and then try to decide how to divide them fairly. They make two piles of six beans each with one left over. One bug refuses to eat the thirteenth bean because he's superstitious. They invite a friend and make three piles of four beans each with one left over. They try a variety of mathematical solutions to split the beans evenly. In the end, they put all of the beans into one bowl and tell their friends to help themselves. Everyone eats a different number of beans according to their different appetites. As you tell the story, have thirteen beans on a table for everyone to see. Split them into piles according to the story. Beanbags, buttons, or other objects can be substitutes for the beans.

Musical Activity

"Ravioli," traditional.

Sing this song to the tune of "Alouette." Many adults in the audience will know the tune "Alouette" and quickly catch on to the call-and-response aspects of the song.

> Ravioli, I like ravioli,
> Ravioli, it's the best for me.
> **Leader**: Have I got it on my chin?   *(point to chin)*
> **Audience**: Yes, you have it on your chin.   *(everyone points to own chin)*
> **Leader**: On my chin?
> **Audience**: On your chin.
> **All**: Oh-oh-oh-oh. Ravioli, I like ravioli,
> Ravioli, it's the best for me.
>
> Ravioli, I like ravioli,
> Ravioli, it's the best for me.
> **Leader**: Have I got it on my shirt?   *(point to shirt)*
> **Audience**: Yes, you have it on your shirt.   *(everyone points to own shirt)*
> **Leader**: On my shirt?
> **Audience**: On your shirt.
> **All**: Oh-oh-oh-oh. Ravioli, I like ravioli,
> Ravioli, it's the best for me.
>
> Ravioli, I like ravioli,
> Ravioli, it's the best for me.
> **Leader**: Have I got it on my shoe?   *(point to shoe)*
> **Audience**: Yes, you have it on your shoe.   *(everyone points to own shoe)*
> **Leader**: On my shoe?
> **Audience**: On your shoe.

All: Oh-oh-oh-oh. Ravioli, I like ravioli,

Ravioli, it's the best for me.

Ravioli, I like ravioli,

Ravioli, it's the best for me.

Leader: Have I got it in my hair?   *(point to hair)*

Audience: Yes, you have it in your hair.   *(everyone points to own hair)*

Leader: In my hair?

Audience: In your hair.

All: Oh-oh-oh-oh. Ravioli, I like ravioli,

Ravioli, it's the best for me.

Continue with pointing to other body parts and articles of clothing. Consider letting members of the audience be the leader.

Picture Book

Yoko, by Rosemary Wells. Hyperion, 1998.

Yoko brings sushi to school for her lunch. The other kids make fun of her food. "Ick! It's green! It's seaweed!" Yoko is upset. At snack time, the process is repeated when Yoko eats red bean ice cream. "Red bean ice cream is for weirdos!" Yoko's teacher decides to have International Food Day. The students bring enchiladas, Caribbean coconut crisps, mango smoothies, Nigerian nut soup, Brazil nuts, spaghetti, potato knishes, Irish stew, and Boston franks and beans. Still, no one eats Yoko's sushi until Timothy eats a crab cone and likes it.

Picture Book

A Birthday Cake Is No Ordinary Cake, by Debra Frasier. Harcourt, 2006.

Directions are given to make a birthday cake. This recipe includes ingredients like the sun, a robin's song, a cool fall morning, the sound of a snowflake falling, and more. The baker directs us to first tie our aprons and put on our hats. Ask the audience to stand and mime these motions. They can be creative when they act out the other commands, such as collecting the first sunrise ("just point your bowl eastward"), circling, "stir in any two bright spring flowers," and catch a falling star. Finally, add regular cake ingredients, such as flour and sugar, lick the spoon, light a candle, sing, wish, and point bowls eastward as the process begins all over again.

Craft Activity

"Paper Plate Cake Clock," by Debra Frasier.

Go to Debra Frasier's website, www.debrafrasier.com/pages/books/bdaycake .html, and find her craft ideas that accompany her book *A Birthday Cake Is No Ordinary Cake.* There are coloring pages, instructions to make baker's hats, and more. The "Paper Plate Cake Clock" pattern can be downloaded and copied for audience members. Supplies are listed on the website as well as photos of family members creating their own paper-plate clocks.

Party/International

"After-Program International Food Day Party"

Well in advance of the program, advertise the program theme and ask folks to bring edible items to share to go along with the picture book *Yoko,* by Rosemary Wells.

MIX AND MATCH

Additional Picture Books

Freymann, Saxton, and Joost Elffers. *How Are You Peeling? Foods with Moods.* **Scholastic, 1999.**

The artists created human-looking faces on a variety of fruits and vegetables. The book discusses the many emotions everyone experiences. "Amused? Confused? Frustrated? Surprised? Try these feelings on for size." Ask the kids to identify each food item as you turn the pages.

Palatini, Margie. *Sweet Tooth.* **Illustrated by Jack E. Davis. Simon & Schuster, 2004.**

Young Stewart has a tooth that constantly makes demands. Everyone blames Stewart when the Sweet Tooth talks. "Move it along, Gramps. Cut the cake." Stewart threatens to put the tooth on a healthy diet. The Sweet Tooth gets quieter and quieter, especially after Stewart brushes and flosses. When the tooth fights back, Stewart chomps on a carrot, and the Sweet Tooth becomes the Tooth Fairy's problem.

Steig, William. *Pete's a Pizza.* **HarperCollins, 1998.**

Pete is in a bad mood because he's stuck indoors on a rainy day. His father cheers him up by pretending that Pete's a pizza. Father sets Pete on a kitchen table and stretches him as if he were dough. He flips him up high, sprinkles oil (water) and flour (talcum powder). Father next adds tomatoes (checkers) and cheese (bits of paper). Father picks up the pizza and bakes it in the oven (the couch). Pete the pizza laughs and runs away because the sun has come out.

Sutton, Jane. *The Trouble with Cauliflower.* Illustrated by Jim Harris. Dial, 2006.

Mortimer is enjoying Sadie's stew until she mentions she added cauliflower to it. Mortimer insists that he has a bad day whenever he eats cauliflower. Indeed, the day after he eats the stew, bad things happen to Mortimer. He fails his driving test and vows to never eat cauliflower again. Sadie and Mortimer dine again. The next day, Mortimer has the best day ever. Sadie informs Mortimer that she had cauliflower in her vegetable surprise casserole and he still had a good day. The two go out for pizza and Mortimer tells them to add cauliflower to it.

Thompson, Lauren. *The Apple Pie That Papa Baked.* Illustrated by Jonathan Bean. Simon & Schuster, 2007.

In a cumulative pattern similar to the classic rhyme "The House That Jack Built," we see the pie that Papa baked. Next, we find "the apples, juicy and red, that went in the pie, warm and sweet, that Papa baked." We also see the tree that grew the apples, the roots that fed the tree, the rain that watered the roots, the clouds that dropped the rain, the sky that carried the clouds, the sun that lit the sky, and the world that spins with the sun.

Wilson, Karma. *Whopper Cake.* Illustrated by Will Hillenbrand. McElderry, 2007.

Granddad plans on making Grandma a whopper of a cake. He adds twenty-three cups of sugar instead of the usual two cups. Instead of four eggs, he adds eighty-six. He mixes the ingredients in the back of a pickup truck. He replaces the mixing spoon with a boat oar. The cake rises ten feet tall. Folks from all over help spread the frosting with shovels. After surprising Grandma, Granddad cleans the dirty dishes in the bathtub.

Additional Songs

"Chilly Chili." From *What's Eatin' Yosi?* by Yosi. Yosi, 2006.

"Five a Day." From *Bon Appétit!* by Cathy Fink and Marcy Marxer. Rounder Records, 2003.

"It's a Pizza." From *Cool to Be in School,* by Stephen Fite. Melody House, 2004.

"Ooey Gooey." From *Ooey Gooey,* by Jim Cosgrove. Hiccup, 2001.

"Peggy's Pie Parlor." From *Peggy's Pie Parlor,* by Ralph's World. Mini Fresh, 2003.

"Victor Vito." From *Victor Vito,* by Laurie Berkner. Two Tomatoes, 1999.

"What I Want Is a Proper Cup of Coffee." From *Family Music Party,* by Trout Fishing in America. Trout, 1998.

Wild Critters

PROGRAM AT A GLANCE

Opening Song: "The Vegetarian Barbeque Moose" from *Toad Motel* by Rick Charette
Picture Book: *Scaredy Squirrel* by Mélanie Watt
Picture Book: *Quiet Night* by Marilyn Singer
Song: "The Bear," traditional
Picture Book: *The Seals on the Bus* by Lenny Hort
Movement Activity: "I'm Driving Along" by Rob Reid
Picture Book/Movement Activity: *Looking for a Moose* by Phyllis Root
Picture Book: *Can You Growl like a Bear?* by John Butler

PREPARATION AND PRESENTATION

Opening Song

"The Vegetarian Barbeque Moose." From *Toad Motel*, by Rick Charette. Pine Point, 1999.

This particular moose likes to put barbeque sauce on its leaves. Adults, in particular, will appreciate the images this song brings up. Charette lives in Maine, where moose and mosquitoes (he sings about those, too) are in great supply.

Picture Book

Scaredy Squirrel, **by Mélanie Watt. Kids Can, 2006.**

A squirrel is afraid to break out of his routine and leave his tree. Bad things can happen. His routine is boring but safe. One day, a bee appears, and

Scaredy Squirrel jumps. He discovers that he's a flying squirrel. When nothing bad happens, he includes jumping "into the unknown" into his daily schedule. Adults, in particular, will enjoy Scaredy Squirrel's emergency plan and emergency kit (which includes bug spray, hard hat, antibacterial soap, calamine lotion, and sardines).

Picture Book

Quiet Night, **by Marilyn Singer. Illustrated by John Manders. Clarion, 2002.**
The audience will have fun making the noises of nocturnal animals. A frog goes "bar-rum," owls go "whoo-hoo," and geese honk. They are joined by fish "whap-slapping," coyotes, raccoons, mice, mosquitoes, and crickets. Human campers finally quiet the cacophony by murmuring, "Turn on the light!" The flashlight momentarily freezes the animals and then sends them scattering.

Song

"The Bear," traditional.
Sing or chant each line of this camp song and have the audience echo each line. Have the audience repeat the previous lines with you as you conclude each stanza. The melody and slightly different lyrics can be found on the recording *Wee Sing Fun 'n' Folk,* by Pamela Beall and Susan Nipp (Price Stern Sloan, 1989).

> The other day,   (The other day,)
> I met a bear,   (I met a bear,)
> Out in the woods,   (Out in the woods,)
> A great big bear.   (A great big bear.)
> **Together**: The other day, I met a bear, out in the woods, a great big bear.
>
> He said to me,   (He said to me,)
> "Why don't you run?   (Why don't you run?)
> "I see you don't   (I see you don't)
> "Have any gun."   (Have any gun.)
> **Together**: He said to me, "Why don't you run? I see you don't have any gun."
>
> And so I ran   (And so I ran)
> Away from there,   (Away from there,)
> And right behind   (And right behind)
> Me was that bear.   (Me was that bear.)
> **Together**: And so I ran away from there, and right behind me was that bear.

Ahead of me,   (Ahead of me,)
I saw a tree,   (I saw a tree,)
A great big tree,   (A great big tree,)
O glory be.   (O glory be.)
Together: Ahead of me, I saw a tree, a great big tree, O glory be.

And so I jumped   (And so I jumped)
Into the air.   (Into the air.)
I missed a branch   (I missed a branch)
Away up there.   (Away up there.)
Together: And so I jumped into the air. I missed a branch away up there.

Now don't you worry,   (Now don't you worry,)
Don't you frown,   (Don't you frown,)
I caught that branch   (I caught that branch)
A-headin' down.   (A-headin' down.)
Together: Now don't you worry, don't you frown, I caught that branch
    a-headin' down.

That's all there is,   (That's all there is,)
There is no more,   (There is no more,)
Until I meet   (Until I meet)
That bear once more.   (That bear once more.)
Together: That's all there is, there is no more, until I meet that bear once
    more.

The end, the end,   (The end, the end,)
The end, the end,   (The end, the end,)
This time it really   (This time it really)
Is the end.   (Is the end.)
Together: The end, the end, the end, the end, this time it really is the end.

Picture Book

The Seals on the Bus, **by Lenny Hort. Illustrated by G. Brian Karas. Holt, 2000.**
When this book came out, I slapped my forehead and said, "Why didn't I
think of this?" The audience will be singing the text to the tune of the traditional

"The Wheels on the Bus." Cue them before each new set of characters appears and let them sing the rest of each verse. The seals on the bus go "errp, errp, errp"; the tiger goes "roar, roar, roar"; the geese go "honk, honk, honk"; the rabbits go up and down; the monkeys go "eeeeh, eeeeh, eeeeh"; the vipers go "hiss, hiss, hiss"; and the sheep go "bah, bah, bah." The skunks upset everyone by going "sssss, sssss, sssss"; and the people on the bus leave screaming "help, help, help!" (At least, the adult humans do. The kids are having a good time.) Encourage the audience to make gestures for the different characters, too. For example, they can clap their hands for the seals, scratch their heads for the monkeys, and hold their noses for the skunks.

Movement Activity

"I'm Driving Along," by Rob Reid.

Face the audience and pretend you're driving a car. Say the little ditty, stop the car, and state that you see a certain animal. The audience becomes that animal and makes movement and sounds associated with that animal. Let them decide how they want to represent the animal. Repeat several times.

> I'm driving along,
> I'm singing a song,
> When suddenly
> I spot a rabbit!
> *(Make sounds and motions of braking the car. Audience members act like rabbits, hopping around, fingers for ears, etc.)*

> I'm driving along,
> I'm singing my song,
> When suddenly
> I spot a wolf!
> *(Stop car. Audience members typically howl.)*

> I'm driving along,
> I'm singing my song,
> When suddenly
> I spot a moose!
> *(Stop car. Audience members may make antlers out of their hands and make chewing motions.)*

Feel free to let a member of the audience shout out what kind of animal they should be. I've also had everyone in the audience drive in the car with me while one volunteer stands apart. That person shouts out what kind of animal he or she is and makes the appropriate sounds and motions. Then someone else gets a turn.

Picture Book/Movement Activity

Looking for a Moose, by Phyllis Root. Illustrated by Randy Cecil. Candlewick, 2006.

A group of children go looking for a moose—"a branchy-antler, dinner-diving, bulgy-nose moose." They venture through the woods, swamp, bushes, and up a hillside. They finally see not one moose but dozens of moose. The picture book has the feel of the traditional story program activity "We're Going on a Bear Hunt." Cue your audience with asides as you read the story. Have everyone pretend to pull on their hats and boots and hike *(slap their legs)*. When everyone gets to the swamp, roll up pants, take off boots, and "squeech squooch" through the muck *(lift feet slowly)*. Roll down pants, button up sleeves, and walk through the bushes *(move palms together)*. Get to the hillside, take off hats, and climb *(huff and lift legs laboriously)*. Everyone makes moose antlers once the moose are spotted (astute young readers will see hints of moose in the illustrations long before the end of the book).

Picture Book

Can You Growl like a Bear? by John Butler. Peachtree, 2007.

Each double-page spread features a different creature making a noise. Bear growls, chimp chatters, dolphin clicks, honeybee buzzes, elephant trumpets, tree frog croaks, leopard roars, cockatoo squawks, wolf howls, and panda snuffles. The book ends with the various animals and birds going to sleep. The volume in the room will rise and settle down as the audience members make the animal noises.

MIX AND MATCH

Additional Picture Books

Banks, Kate. *Fox.* Illustrated by Georg Hallensleben. Farrar, Straus & Giroux, 2007.

A fox is born in the spring. As he grows, he asks his parents, "When will I be ready?" His parents tell him he's not ready yet. First, he must learn the ways of the forest, how to hunt and find berries, and what to do when the enemy is nearby. The seasons change and the fox sticks close to his parents. When the time comes, the fox leaves, and "the mama fox knows and the papa fox too that he will be fine."

Butler, John. *Ten in the Den.* **Peachtree, 2005.**

Ten different types of woodland mammals act out the traditional song "Ten in the Bed." The little mouse tells the other animals to "Roll over! Roll over!" They all roll over, and Rabbit falls out of the den to the bottom of a hill. Rabbit is joined by Mole, Beaver, Badger, Porcupine, Raccoon, Fox, Squirrel, and Bear. Mouse misses his friends and rolls down to meet them. Sing the text; the audience will join in.

Melling, David. *The Scallywags.* **Barron's, 2006.**

The animals are tired of the wolves' poor behavior. The wolves try to change their slovenly ways. They take baths, dress nicely, and improve their manners. The wolves' standards become so high that they insult the other animals. The wolves revert back to their old selves when the full moon comes out. The other animals accept the wolves for what they are and party through the night.

Rex, Michael. *Dunk Skunk.* **Putnam, 2005.**

This short sports book consists of animal-name rhymes. A "Goal Mole" defends a soccer net. A "Freestyle Crocodile" makes a sharp turn on a skateboard. "Cheer Deer" wave pom-poms at the game. After reading the book, ask the audience members to come up with more animal-action rhymes.

Van Fleet, Matthew. *Tails.* **Harcourt, 2003.**

Here's a good tactile-toy book to have in the story program area for families to inspect before and after the program. Van Fleet adds many types of material to replicate the feel of animal tails. There are plenty of flaps to flip and tabs to pull, also. There's even a scratch-and-sniff feature on the skunk's tail! Featured animals include foxes, pandas, chipmunks, alligators, weasels, pangolins, and more. The final flap unfolds to show all of the animals on the back of "the biggest tail of all"—that of a whale.

Weeks, Sarah. *If I Were a Lion.* **Illustrated by Heather M. Solomon. Atheneum, 2004.**

A little girl is punished and put in her time-out chair. Her mother says, "I do not like it when you're wild." The girl imagines acting wild like a lion, scaring the cat, or a bear, ripping the pillows. She thinks what it would be like to be a wolf, frog, alligator, mountain goat, whale, rhino, and more. The girl realizes "the opposite of wild is . . . me."

Wilson, Karma. *Bear Wants More.* **Illustrated by Jane Chapman. McElderry, 2003.**

Bear wakes up extremely hungry. He nibbles on grass, "but the bear wants more!" Teach the audience to say this refrain as Bear continues his search for food. Mouse joins Bear for berries, Hare takes Bear to the clover patch, and Badger goes fishing with Bear. Still, Bear wants more. More animals join them and throw Bear a party. By now Bear has eaten so much that he's too large to fit back in his den.

Additional Songs

"Bring Back the Bat." From *I'm All Ears: Sing into Reading,* by Fran Avni. Starfish Music, 1999.

"Grey Squirrel." From *Sing It! Say It! Stamp It! Sway It!* vol. 3, by Peter and Ellen Allard. 80-Z Music, 2002.

"I'm Proud to Be a Beaver." From *Goin' Wild,* by the Banana Slug String Band. Slug Music, 1999.

"Mole in the Ground." From *One More River,* by Bill Staines. Red House, 1998.

"Night Creatures." From *Singing Science,* by Tickle Tune Typhoon. Music for Little People, 2000.

"Ooh There's a Lion." From *Kimmy Schwimmy Music,* vol. 1, by Kimmy Schwimmy. North Corner, 2005.

Winter Wonderland

PROGRAM AT A GLANCE

Opening Song: "So Cold Outside" from *Tuning into Nature* by Fran Avni

Picture Book: *Duck at the Door* by Jackie Urbanovic

Picture Book/Felt Board: *Sleep, Black Bear, Sleep* by Jane Yolen and Heidi E. Y. Stemple

Musical Activity: "Does Your Scarf Hang Low?" traditional; adapted by Rob Reid

Picture Book: *Winter Is the Warmest Season* by Lauren Stringer

Musical Activity: "If You're Happy and You Know It—Winter Style," traditional; adapted by Rob Reid

Picture Book: *Straight to the Pole* by Kevin O'Malley

Movement Activity: "Snowball" by Rob Reid

Picture Book: *Snow Sounds: An Onomatopoeic Story* by David A. Johnson

PREPARATION AND PRESENTATION

Opening Song

"So Cold Outside." From *Tuning into Nature*, by Fran Avni. Lemonstone, 2002.

Folks will want to cover up when they hear Avni shiver and sing "Brr—it's cold outside." This song is perfect to set the tone for the program theme. Avni is an expert in developing reading-readiness songs and activities for children.

Picture Book

Duck at the Door, by Jackie Urbanovic. HarperCollins, 2007.

Max the duck stays behind when his flock heads south for the winter. He knocks at Irene's home, and she welcomes the duck to stay for the winter with her and her menagerie. Max makes himself at home and soon irritates the other animals (especially when he hogs the television remote). The other animals are also tired of the duck's recipes, such as "Max's Tofu Surprise" and "Max's Seaweed Chowder." Spring arrives, and Max is reunited with his flock. Irene and her animals find themselves missing Max. Max returns the following winter—with the rest of his flock.

Picture Book/Felt Board

Sleep, Black Bear, Sleep, by Jane Yolen and Heidi E. Y. Stemple. Illustrated by Brooke Dyer. HarperCollins, 2007.

Light verse describes various anthropomorphic animals that hibernate or are fairly inactive during the winter months. These include the black bear, frog, bat, snake, box turtle, gopher, skunk, badger, beaver, mouse, toad, and chipmunk. Make felt characters of each animal ahead of time and ask various children to place the characters on the board as you read each little poem.

Musical Activity

"Does Your Scarf Hang Low?" traditional; adapted by Rob Reid.

Bring several scarves and have members of the audience put them on and do the motions with you. If you have a large audience, ask the few with scarves to join you in front. Place your scarf around your neck and move the ends to the lyrics as you sing. Sing to the tune of "Do Your Ears Hang Low?"

> Does your scarf hang low?
> Does it wobble to and fro?
> Can you tie it in a knot?
> Can you tie it in a bow?
> Can you throw it over your shoulder
> Like a Continental soldier?
> Does your scarf hang low?

Picture Book

Winter Is the Warmest Season, **by Lauren Stringer. Harcourt, 2006.**

A young boy states that winter is warm because that's the season he wears heavy clothing, eats hot foods, sits in front of the fireplace, takes warm baths, and cuddles with his pets and stuffed animals. Bodies also sit close together to share stories. As he lies in bed buried under the warm covers, he imagines "I might dream of summer . . . just to cool me off!"

Musical Activity

"If You're Happy and You Know It—Winter Style," traditional; adapted by Rob Reid.

Ask everyone to stand and mime the actions to this popular, traditional song.

If you're happy and you know it, clap your mittens.
If you're happy and you know it, clap your mittens.
If you're happy and you know it and you really want to show it,
If you're happy and you know it, clap your mittens.

If you're happy and you know it, twirl your scarves.
If you're happy and you know it, twirl your scarves.
If you're happy and you know it and you really want to show it,
If you're happy and you know it, twirl your scarves.

If you're happy and you know it, stomp your boots.
If you're happy and you know it, stomp your boots.
If you're happy and you know it and you really want to show it,
If you're happy and you know it, stomp your boots.

If you're happy and you know it, throw a snowball.
If you're happy and you know it, throw a snowball.
If you're happy and you know it and you really want to show it,
If you're happy and you know it, throw a snowball.

If you're happy and you know it, make a snow angel.
If you're happy and you know it, make a snow angel.
If you're happy and you know it and you really want to show it,
If you're happy and you know it, make a snow angel.

Picture Book

Straight to the Pole, by Kevin O'Malley. Walker, 2003.

Adults will particularly enjoy seeing the images of a young child bravely facing the elements knee-deep in snow. The storm is getting worse, and the child thinks that he can't go on. He stumbles and asks us to remember him—right before we realize he has crawled to a bus-stop sign and is joined by his dog and friends. The atmosphere changes to joy when he learns that school has been canceled. Ask the audience to make howling-wind noises as the young narrator exaggerates his trek.

Movement Activity

"Snowball," by Rob Reid.

This was inspired by the camp call-and-response chant "Flea Fly Mosquito." Ask the audience members if they ever had the experience of snow down their backs. For those folks living in warmer climes, ask them to imagine an ice cube running down the back of their shirts. Ask them to stand and repeat after each line.

> Snow!   (Snow!)
>
> Snowball!   (Snowball!)
>
> Slushy-wushy snowball!   (Slushy-wushy snowball!)
>
> Slushy-wushy snowball sliding down my neck!   (Slushy-wushy snowball sliding down my neck!)
>
> *(Look panicked and slap at back of neck.)*
>
> Slushy-wushy snowball sliding down my back!   (Slushy-wushy snowball sliding down my back!)
>
> *(Slap at back.)*
>
> Ooh it's cold, it's oh-so-cold, this snowball down my back!   (Ooh it's cold, it's oh-so-cold, this snowball down my back!)
>
> *(Hop around.)*
>
> Cold-cold, cold-cold-cold, oh, it's really cold!   (Cold-cold, cold-cold-cold, oh, it's really cold!)
>
> *(Dance wildly in circles with arms flailing.)*
>
> Oh! *(pause)* It's not cold anymore.   (Oh! [*pause*] It's not cold anymore.)
>
> *(Stop and shrug shoulders.)*

Picture Book

Snow Sounds: An Onomatopoeic Story, by David A. Johnson. Houghton Mifflin, 2006.

The entire text consists of winter noises and is perfect as a call-and-response piece. Ask the audience to repeat each word you say as they see the various winter pictures. A child snores, a cat purrs, a snowplow drives by with a "Swoosh Slush Smoosh." Another plow goes by with a "Crash Crush Clank" and backs up with "beep beep beep beep." A snowblower is at work while the child eats breakfast. The sidewalk is scraped shortly before the school bus arrives with a "Honk Honk."

MIX AND MATCH

Additional Picture Books

Butler, M. Christina. *One Winter's Day.* **Illustrated by Tina Macnaughton. Good Books, 2006.**

Little Hedgehog is having trouble keeping warm. He puts on his hat, scarf, and mittens before heading to Badger's home. Along the way, he finds a family of field mice huddling in the cold. He gives them his woolly hat. He next comes across Otter, who is "huffing and puffing on his paws" to keep warm. Little Hedgehog gives Otter his mittens. He next finds a fawn shivering in the cold and gives the deer his scarf. He finally arrives at Badger's all rolled up in a snowball. The two return to Little Hedgehog's home after the winter storm. They find his nest rebuilt and decorated with his mittens, scarf, and hat.

Hogg, Gary. *Look What the Cat Dragged In!* **Illustrated by Mike Wohnoutka. Dutton, 2005.**

The inhabitants of Lazybone Cabin are cold from the harsh winter. They threaten to skin the cat to make quilts and slippers. The frightened cat sneaks out and drags back plenty of firewood. The ungrateful inhabitants complain about the lack of food and discuss eating the cat. The cat rushes out and returns with a sled full of fast-food items. After filling their stomachs, the family grows bored and thinks of games that "torture" the cat, such as pin the tail on the cat. The cat finds game boards and toys. When the complaining troupe discusses selling the cat, the cat runs out and returns with bags of money. The cat is fed up when they talk about buying a dog. He returns with the law and others (the cat stole everything), and the Lazybone Cabin folks are hauled off to jail.

Hubbell, Will. *Snow Day Dance.* **Whitman, 2005.**

Schoolchildren make snowflakes and whisper about the possibility of a snow day. The next morning, "the radio says, 'All schools closed.'" The children play outside. They examine the snowflakes, make snowmen, and head for the sledding hill. They see a strange shape through the falling snow. It turns out to be their "teacher doing the snowy day dance!"

Hurst, Carol Otis. *Terrible Storm.* **Illustrated by S. D. Schindler. Greenwillow, 2007.**

Adults like to talk about the old days. Things were different back then. Even the storms were more terrible. Two old men recall a particular three-day storm that hit when they were younger. Ask an adult in the audience to read this book with you. The text and illustrations are split into the two voices.

Pulver, Robin. *Axle Annie.* **Illustrated by Tedd Arnold. Dial, 1999.**

Axle Annie is a modern tall-tale character who drives the school bus. She never fails to deliver the kids to school, even on the snowiest days. She always makes it up Tiger Hill, and "that's why the schools in Burskyville never had a snow day." This makes Shifty Rhodes, another bus driver, angry. He wants a snow day. He plots to add even more snow to Tiger Hill with a snowmaking machine. Axle Annie finds that she needs help with this challenge.

Additional Songs

"The Earth Is Still Sleeping." From *Waltzing with Fireflies,* from Elizabeth McMahon. Rosie Rhubarb, 1999.

"I Can Make a Snowman." From *H.U.M.—All Year Long,* by Carole Peterson. Macaroni Soup, 2003.

"I'm a Little Snowflake." From *Whaddaya Think of That?* by Laurie Berkner. Two Tomatoes, 2000.

"Smells like Winter." From *Do You Wish You Could Fly?* by Kathy Byers. KT Music, 2000.

"Snowflakes." From *Seasonal Songs in Motion,* by the Learning Station. Monopoli/Learning Station, 2001.

"Winter's Come and Gone." From *You Are My Little Bird,* by Elizabeth Mitchell. Smithsonian Folkways, 2006.

Woof and Wag

PROGRAM AT A GLANCE

Opening Song: "Alice the Beagle" from *Sing-a-Move-a-Dance* by Colleen and
    Uncle Squaty
Picture Book: *The Best Pet of All* by David LaRochelle
Picture Book: *Widget* by Lyn Rossiter McFarland
Movement Activity: "I Have Fleas" by Rob Reid
Picture Book: *Bark, George* by Jules Feiffer
Song: "Bingo's Friends," traditional; adapted by Rob Reid
Picture Book/Movement Activity: *Move Over, Rover!* by Karen Beaumont
Sound-Effects Activity: "My Dog Is a Noisy Dog" by Rob Reid
Picture Book/Movement Activity: *Wiggle* by Doreen Cronin

PREPARATION AND PRESENTATION

Opening Song

**"Alice the Beagle." From *Sing-a-Move-a-Dance*, by Colleen and Uncle Squaty.
Colleen and Uncle Squaty, 2005.**

    The antics of Alice will set the tone for this lively story program. Kids and
parents will hear about Alice's encounter with kittens that make her puff up, stamp
her feet, bark real loud, and wag her tail. Colleen Hannafin and Brian Schellinger
make up this award-winning musical duo from Wisconsin.

Picture Book

The Best Pet of All, by David LaRochelle. Illustrated by Hanako Wakiyama. Dutton, 2004.

A boy asks his mother if he could have a dog. His mother replies that dogs are too messy. The boy asks if he could have a dragon, and the amused mother says, "If you can find a dragon, you can keep it for a pet." The boy finds a dragon at the drugstore. The dragon, however, turns out to be very messy and won't go away. The boy suggests to his mother that dragons don't like dogs. A dog shows up and the dragon leaves, but not before giving the boy the high-five sign. Were the two in on the plan from the beginning?

Picture Book

Widget, by Lyn Rossiter McFarland. Illustrated by Jim McFarland. Farrar, Straus & Giroux, 2001.

Widget is a stray dog who wanders into a house with an old woman and her six cats. The cats, also known as "the girls," don't like dogs. Widget pretends that he is a cat by meowing, puffing up, hissing and spitting, purring, playing with a toy mouse, and using the litter box. They all get along as cats until the woman falls down, injuring herself. Widget starts barking for help. The cats are stunned by Widget's true identity, but then they start barking, too.

Movement Activity

"I Have Fleas," by Rob Reid.

The audience can do this starting in a sitting position.

> I'm a dog and I have fleas,
> I have to scratch my ears. Arrrooooo! *(scratch behind ears with left hand and howl)*

> I'm a dog and I have fleas,
> I have to scratch my back *(scratch back with right hand)*
> and ears *(scratch)*. Arrrooooo! *(howl)*

> I'm a dog and I have fleas,
> I have to scratch my leg *(pretend to bite one leg)*
> and back *(scratch)* and ears *(scratch)*. Arrrooooo! *(howl)*

I'm a dog and I have fleas,

I have to scratch my rear *(stand and wiggle hips)*

And leg *(bite)* and back *(scratch)* and ears *(scratch).* Arrrooooo! *(howl)*

Thank goodness! *(come to a complete stop)*

I think they are gone! *(slowly, give a little scratch behind one ear)*

Picture Book

Bark, George, by Jules Feiffer. HarperCollins, 1999.

George's mother tells her puppy to bark. George meows, then quacks, oinks, and moos. George's mother takes him to the vet. The vet reaches down George's throat and pulls out a cat, then a duck, a pig, and a cow. George is then able to bark. The next time George's mother asks him to bark, he says, "Hello." Ask the audience members to make the appropriate animal noises with George.

Song

"Bingo's Friends," traditional; adapted by Rob Reid.

Sing the first verse of the traditional song "B-I-N-G-O."

There was a farmer had a dog and Bingo was his name-o.

B-I-N-G-O, B-I-N-G-O, B-I-N-G-O, and Bingo was his name-o.

Then ask the audience members to shout out their pet dogs' names or names of dogs they know. Alter the verse slightly by changing the word *farmer* to *family*. The rhythm will also change depending on the number of letters in the dog names. Half the fun is trying to rush the longer names into the pattern. For example, here was a dog name that came up when I led this song at a family school night.

There was a family had a dog and Lilly Belle was her name-o,

L-I-L-L-Y-B-E-L-L-E, L-I-L-L-Y-B-E-L-L-E, L-I-L-L-Y-B-E-L-L-E, and
Lilly Belle was her name-o.

The trick is to sing most of the letters in a fairly monotone delivery and sing the last letter of the name in the right pitch that matches the traditional song. Most dog names aren't quite as challenging. In the next example, for Fluffy, put a brief pause between the *u* and the following *f.*

There was a family had a dog and Fluffy was his name-o.

F-L-U-F-F-Y, F-L-U-F-F-Y, F-L-U-F-F-Y, and Fluffy was his name-o.

Consider using famous literary dogs, such as Shiloh, Snoopy, Walter, Susan Meddaugh's Martha, or Clifford, the Big Red Dog.

> There was a family read a book and Clifford was his name-o.
>
> C-L-I-F-F-O-R-D, C-L-I-F-F-O-R-D, C-L-I-F-F-O-R-D, and Clifford was
> his name-o.

Picture Book/Movement Activity

Move Over, Rover! **by Karen Beaumont. Illustrated by Jane Dyer. Harcourt, 2006.**

Rover is sleeping in his doghouse when a storm arrives. Several animals crowd into the doghouse with Rover. The last animal in is Skunk. The other animals leave in a hurry. Rover finally gets his house back when the storm ends. Have different audience members act out this cumulative-pattern story while you read the book. You need someone to play Rover the dog, a cat, a raccoon, a squirrel, a blue jay, a snake, a mouse, and a skunk. If you have a small audience, then you can simply read the story without actors and have them make sound effects of the storm. Designate a small circle to represent the doghouse. The actors have to crowd into the circle one by one. The rest of the audience can provide the storm sound effects.

Sound-Effects Activity

"My Dog Is a Noisy Dog," by Rob Reid.

Ask everyone to make the following dog noises with you.

> My dog is a noisy dog,
> He barks and barks all day.   *(bark)*
>
> My dog is a noisy dog,
> He growls and growls all day.   *(growl)*
>
> My dog is a noisy dog,
> He whines and whines all day.   *(whine)*
>
> My dog is a noisy dog,
> He pants and pants all day.   *(pant)*
>
> My dog is a noisy dog,
> He slurps and slurps all day.   *(slurp)*

My dog is a noisy dog,

He snores and snores all day—and night!   *(snore)*

Picture Book/Movement Activity

Wiggle, by Doreen Cronin. Illustrated by Scott Menchin. Atheneum, 2005.

A dog shows off a series of movements. The dog wiggles upon waking, wiggles with his breakfast, wiggles his hair, and "wiggles where your tail would be." He imagines what it's like to wiggle with gorillas, fish, a crocodile, bees, snakes, and polar bears. At the very end of the book, the dog says, "Would you join me for a wiggle?" Lead the audience in series of wiggles, and while they are still wiggling, read the final lines. "I think we're out of wiggles now. See you wiggle soon!"

MIX AND MATCH

Additional Picture Books

Casanova, Mary. *Some Dog!* Illustrated by Ard Hoyt. Farrar, Straus & Giroux, 2007.

George is a dog having a comfortable life until a lively stray dog named Zippity joins the household. Everyone is amazed by Zippity's energy and talents. Everyone, that is, except George. George is worn out by Zippity's antics. A thunderstorm arrives, and Zippity panics and runs away. It's up to George to rescue the small dog.

Jenkins, Emily. *That New Animal.* Illustrated by Pierre Pratt. Farrar, Straus & Giroux, 2005.

FudgeFudge and Marshmallow don't like the new animal (a newborn human baby). Their owners don't pay attention to the two dogs anymore. One day, "someone else arrives. They call him Grandpa." When the new person heads toward the baby, the dogs bark "until the Grandpa goes and sits on the other side of the room." The two dogs now feel very protective of the "new animal."

Joosse, Barbara. *Bad Dog School.* Illustrated by Jennifer Plecas. Clarion, 2004.

Zippy is a high-energy dog. His young owner, Harris, loves Zippy. The rest of the family is worn out and sends Zippy to obedience school. Zippy returns a changed dog, but the family misses the old Zippy. They decide to send him to "Bad Dog School," a school designed by Harris to reteach Zippy some of his old habits in moderation.

Postgate, Daniel. *Smelly Bill.* North South, 2007.

Bill the dog rolls around in smelly garbage and muddy ponds. Great-Aunt Bleach shows up and cleans "the house from tip to toe." She smells Bill and says,

"It's bathie-wathie time for you!" Bill is caught and thrown into the bathtub. He escapes and jumps into the compost bin. Great-Aunt Bleach jumps in after him and is now the one who stinks.

Walton, Rick. *Bertie Was a Watchdog*. Illustrated by Arthur Robins. Candlewick, 2002.

Bertie is a teeny-tiny dog. A robber breaks into the house and laughs at the notion of Bertie being a watchdog. Bertie tries biting the robber, but the bad guy says, "I think I felt a fly kiss my leg." He tries chasing the robber but is ridiculed. Bertie tricks the robber into barking loud enough to attract the attention of the police.

Yaccarino, Dan. *Unlovable*. Holt, 2001.

Alfred is a small pug who is made fun of by a cat, a parrot, a goldfish, and several dogs. "You've got the ugliest mug I've ever seen. No one could love you!" Rex, a golden retriever, moves in next door. Alfred and Rex talk through the fence because it's too high to see each other. When Rex digs a hole under the fence, Alfred learns that Rex is really another pug. The two play together, "and Alfred never felt unlovable again."

Additional Songs

"Don't Listen to My Dog." From *Trash Can*, by Eric Ode. Deep Rooted Music, 2002.

"The Great Big Dog." From *Whaddaya Think of That?* by Laurie Berkner. Two Tomatoes, 2000.

"I Love That Dog." From *A Poodle in Paris*, by Connie Kaldor. Folle Avoine, 2004.

"My Dog." From *A Kid like You*, by Brian Kinder. Brian Kinder, 2002.

"My Little Puppy." From *Martian Television Invasion*, by Thaddeus Rex. Thaddeus Rex, 2005.

"The Tale of a Dog." From *Mouse Jamboree*, by Mary Kaye. Mary Kaye Music, 2004.

A Final Good-bye Activity

In the first *Family Storytime*, I added an original good-bye activity called "A Round of Applause" that could be used for any of the story program themes. I wrote another farewell activity for this book titled "Air Good-bye." The idea came from kids wanting to give me high fives after a program. My hands hurt after a dozen or so slaps, so I resorted to narrowly missing slapping their hands and saying out loud, "Air high five!"

"Air Good-bye" by Rob Reid

> Let's play air guitar, *(mime playing guitar)*
> Let's give an air high five, *(mime giving high fives, not touching hands)*
> Let's give an air kiss, *(blow a silent kiss with a wave of the hand)*
> Let's give an air good-bye. *(wave hands and say "Good-bye")*

Resources

At the time this book was written, all of the children's trade books listed in *More Family Storytimes* were in print and available for purchase through regular vendors. Most children's recordings listed are available through major online bookstores, such as Amazon.com and Barnesandnoble.com. Many are also available through the following web stores:

CD Baby: www.cdbaby.com
Children's Music Hall of Fame: www.childrensmusichalloffame.com
KiddoMusic: www.kiddomusic.com
North Side Music: www.northsidemusicwi.com
Songs for Teaching: www.songsforteaching.com

The following artists are mentioned in *More Family Storytimes* and sell their products through their personal websites:

Abell, Timmy: www.timmyabell.com
Allard, Peter and Ellen: www.peterandellen.com
Alsop, Peter: www.peteralsop.com
Avni, Fran: www.franavni.com
Banana Slug String Band: www.bananaslugstringband.com
Beall, Pamela, and Susan Nipp: www.weesing.com
Berkner, Laurie: www.twotomatoes.com
Big Jeff: www.bigjeffmusic.com
Byers, Kathy: www.kathybyers.com
Chapin, Tom: http://members.aol.com/chapinfo/tc/index.html
Charette, Rick: www.pinepoint.com/rick.html

Coffey, James: www.jamescoffey.com

Colleen and Uncle Squaty: www.colleenandunclesquaty.com

Cosgrove, Jim: www.jimcosgrove.com

Crow, Dan: www.dancrow.com

Daddy A Go Go: www.daddyagogo.com

Dana: www.swiggleditties.com

Fink, Cathy, and Marcy Marxer: www.cathymarcy.com

Fite, Stephen: www.melodyhousemusic.com

Frasier, Debra: www.debrafrasier.com/pages/books/bdaycake.html

Frezza, Rebecca: www.bigtruckmusic.com

Greg and Steve: www.gregandsteve.com

Grunsky, Jack: www.jackgrunsky.com

Harley, Bill: www.billharley.com

Harper, Jessica: www.jessicaharper.com

Harper, Monty: www.montyharper.com

Howdy, Buck: www.buckhowdy.com

Jonas, Billy: www.billyjonas.com

Kaldor, Connie: www.conniekaldor.com

Kaye, Mary: www.marykayemusic.com

Kimmy Schwimmy: www.kimmyschwimmy.com

Kinder, Brian: www.kindersongs.com

Kirk, John, and Trish Miller: www.johnandtrish.com

Knight, Tom: www.tomknight.com

The Learning Station: www.learningstationmusic.com

John Lithgow: www.johnlithgow.com

Ken Lonnquist: www.kenland.com

McMahon, Elizabeth: www.mrsmcpuppet.com

Milkshake: www.milkshakemusic.com

Miss Amy: www.missamykids.com

Mitchell, Elizabeth: www.youaremyflower.org

Ode, Eric: www.ericode.com

Old Town School of Folk Music: www.oldtownschool.org

Parachute Express: www.parachuteexpress.com

Pease, Tom: www.tompease.com

Peterson, Carole: www.macaronisoup.com

Polisar, Barry Louis: www.barrylou.com

Pullara, Steve: www.coolbeansmusic.com

Ralph's World: www.ralphsworld.com
Roberts, Justin: www.justinroberts.org
Rosen, Gary: www.garyrosenkidsmusic.com
Rosenthal, Phil: www.americanmelody.com
Rudnick, Ben: www.benrudnickandfriends.com
Rymer, Brady: www.bradyrymer.com
Shepard, Aaron: www.aaronshep.com
Shontz, Bill: www.billshontz.com
Silberg, "Miss Jackie": www.jackiesilberg.com
Staines, Bill: www.acousticmusic.com/staines/
Stevesongs: www.stevesongs.com
Stotts, Stuart: www.stuartstotts.com
Thaddeus Rex: www.thaddeusrex.com
Tickle Tune Typhoon: www.tickletunetyphoon.com
Trout Fishing in America: www.troutmusic.com
Walker, Graham: www.grahamwalker.ca
Willems, Mo: www.mowillems.com
Yosi: www.yosimusic.com
Zanes, Dan: www.danzanes.com

Index

You may also be interested in the following books from Rob Reid:

Children's Jukebox, Second Edition: This must-have reference doubles the number of musical recordings from the first edition with selections sorted into 170 subject headings, plus subcategories. These nearly 550 children's recordings include Parents Choice Award winners, ALA Notable Recordings, Grammy Award winners, and more.

Something Musical Happened at the Library: Drawing on thousands of hours listening and programming, Reid selects the best of the best, presenting eight ready-to-use, comprehensive lesson plans to help you make music an everyday part of your programs.

Cool Story Programs for the School-Age Crowd: What kid wouldn't love literary explorations of the stinky, creepy, and dirty? Throw in rats, witches, aliens, and underwear and it's irresistible. This proven, adaptable resource is for anyone who wants to help literature come alive for kids in grades K–4.

Something Funny Happened at the Library: This book will serve as your personal humor coach for even the toughest audiences, from enthusiastic preschoolers to unimpressed teens. This complete resource gets children and young adults laughing in the stacks with innovative programming that helps you make the library the hippest place in town!

For more information, please visit www.alastore.ala.org.